BITTER SWEET

T0182685

BITTER SWEET

A True
Story
of Love
and Loss

Lotte Bowser

Text copyright © 2024 by Lotte Bowser
All rights reserved.

No part of this book may be reproduced, or stored in a retrieval system, or transmitted in any form or by any means, electronic, mechanical, photocopying, recording, or otherwise, without express written permission of the publisher.

Published by Little A, Seattle

www.apub.com

Amazon, the Amazon logo, and Little A are trademarks of Amazon.com, Inc., or its affiliates.

ISBN-13: 9781662521409
eISBN: 9781662521416

Cover design and illustration by James Jones

Printed in the United States of America

For Ben.
I am you, you are me, and even in death,
we are still we.

Introduction

It's the golden hour here in Lisbon. Streaks of candyfloss pink paint the sky as the sun begins its descent over the rooftops. I press 'Send' on the email containing the final manuscript of this book to my editors, and sink back into my chair. Tears threaten to soak my cheeks, and I find myself blinking hard against the sting. *If only she could see herself now*, I think – 'she' being the version of me the day that Ben died. There are some people who leave an indelible mark on you. Your life, because of theirs, will never be the same as it was before. Ben was that person for me. He was, or should I say *is*, my person.

At the time of writing this, almost three years have passed since he left. If you'd said to me that I would still be here, and that I'd have found meaning by way of writing a book, I wouldn't have believed you. I was almost certain that the pain of his death would kill me. My grief was like a wildfire, the way it raged and consumed. All I could do was survive the next moment, until a moment became a day, which became a week. Until that week became months, which became years.

My life, this book, is my version of making the impossible possible. In the early aftermath of his death, it took a staggering amount of energy to even run a brush through my hair and put a clean pair of knickers on. I could barely leave my bed. As time passed though, I noticed something remarkable happen. My grief began to loosen its grip. I started to recognise glimpses of the version of myself before cancer, Covid and death consumed her. Chinks of light got in. I put pen to paper and poured my pain into writing. I read countless books about loss, near-death experiences, mediumship and signs. I found a therapist, talked a lot, and built a community of grievers all over the world on social media. I moved abroad, fell in love again, and made best friends for life. Slowly but surely, I stitched up the hole his death had carved out inside of me. The threads still snag and come loose sometimes – all it takes is hearing a joke I know he would've found funny, or a song I know he would've loved. Maybe it's the brand of his favourite crisps, or the smell of Dutch gouda in the grocery shop at the bottom of my road. But those threads don't unravel like they used to. Nowadays, I think of him and I smile to myself. I remember an incredible man who loved me, whose life changed mine for the better.

Some people say that grief is love, but I don't believe that's true. Love isn't supposed to hurt that much. I think grief is a reflection of the love we feel, only now we can't give it to the person it was intended for. It would make sense then, for grief to last as long as love lasts. Personally, I'm okay with that. If you asked me whether I'd do it all again knowing what the outcome would be, my answer would be yes – a thousand times yes. It is better to have loved and lost Ben, than to have never loved him at all. My grief is a consequence of that love. It's a reminder of my improbable life and my inescapable death – an invitation to live with more gratitude for all that *is*. And there are countless things to be grateful for, by the way. My health, the warmth of the early-evening sun on my skin. The fact that I even get to write this book – a once-upon-a-pipe-dream scribbled in a notepad – and actually call it my job.

The book is my story of losing the person I couldn't live without, and learning to do just that. For the purposes of clarity and brevity, there are many valued friends and people of significance who do not appear in it, and I've changed the names of some out of respect for their privacy. There were countless others who knew and loved Ben, but that is their story to tell, not mine. It's not an easy read at times. I considered watering it down and making it more palatable, but instead I have chosen to share every ugly, agonising and sacred part. Why? Because life is beautiful, but it's often difficult and painful too – to have done less would have meant denying what it is to be human. It certainly wasn't easy to write either. In fact, it was one of the hardest things I think I've ever done. I'd told myself time and time again that I couldn't do it. I procrastinated, searched for every last reason not to sit down and type. I was terrified to confront the chunks of time that, until recently, I couldn't seem to account for, to unearth the painful memories I'd buried. I'd hoped that, with enough distance between us, I might be able to forget about them one day, but I've since learned that trauma doesn't work like that. It isn't just an event that happened sometime in the past, nor is it something primarily relating to memory – a story of what happened. Rather, it is the imprint left by that experience on the mind, brain, and body. It can cause our declarative memory system – the ability to store and retrieve personal information such as names, dates, places, events, facts, and so on – to fail. As a result, the traumatic memories aren't logged and stored properly. Our brain encodes the memories as fragmented pictures or sensations instead, which can become sticking points that disrupt our mental and physical processes and give rise to post-traumatic stress symptoms. Only when the memories are properly integrated can we begin to truly heal.

Unearthing those memories has felt excruciating at times. It has forced me to sit with the finality of Ben's death, the cruelty and sheer impossibility of it all, day in and day out. It has forced me to accept my mortality and that of everybody else I love. But as words grew to become lines, and as lines pages, I let the pieces of my story unfurl, stretch out, take up space. In doing so, the pain, I noticed, no longer pressed against the seams of my skin like it used to. It took on a different shape. On the other side of all that resistance was something profound – a catharsis of some kind. *Healing*. To hold this book in my hands, to run my fingers through its pages knowing I have crystallised his legacy and our love into something tangible, will be the second most meaningful thing I've ever done with my life, after walking him to the end of his.

Maybe you see pieces of your own story in mine, maybe you don't. Either way, my wish for you is that by reading this, you are reminded of your own power. Too often we're quick to disempower ourselves on the basis that we 'can't'. Believe me when I say I told myself a million times that I couldn't either. But it's simply not true. You *can*. You can survive things you never thought you'd be capable of surviving. You can do things you never imagined being able to do. I know because I've done it myself. Your experiences will shape you, yes – that much is certain. But they don't have to define who you are. You can rebuild your life from ruin. You can plant seeds in the soil that buried you that can stand tall as flowers one day, with their faces turned to the sun. In Japanese culture, the art of kintsugi uses lacquer dusted with gold to mend broken pottery. Once the pottery has been mended, it's thought to be even more valuable and beautiful. I think that's an incredible metaphor for the indomitability of the human spirit, don't you? It teaches us an important lesson: that while life is indeed fragile – that things can and *do* fall apart – that 'broken' does not necessarily mean beyond repair. In time, we can put our broken pieces back together again. We can make alchemy from our pain; we can find beauty in our scars.

I suppose I ought to clarify what I mean by healing. Healing isn't about reaching an invisible finish line where we clap our hands and declare ourselves fixed for evermore. That isn't a thing, because we aren't before-and-after stories. We are human beings, continually ebbing and flowing and learning and changing. Some days we take ten steps forward, some days we stand still, and other days we take ten steps back. Healing isn't about bypassing our pain, pretending it doesn't exist. Healing is about reaching a place where we are able to carry it, while also growing around it. It's about making more space for hope, curiosity – even joy. I want you to imagine a box with a ball inside it for a moment. The box represents life and the ball represents the pain. At first, the ball takes up all the space inside the box. As time passes, the box grows bigger, creating more space around the ball. It's not that our pain necessarily diminishes in size – it's that the box around it expands. Ben's death cut canyons of sorrow into the landscape of my soul, deep and high and vast. If there is space for all that pain, then there is space for all that is good and beautiful too. How incredible it is to feel so immensely, to have a heart capable of loving so much.

Healing is going to demand a lot from you. It takes work. Courage – and that courage is not always the 'beating your chest and roaring at the top of the mountain' kind. It is also the quiet resolve at the end of a day you thought you'd never get through. It is making a commitment to yourself, while you're curled around the toilet bowl on the bathroom floor, to not give up. Think about it – you have lived through all of your worst days until now, and that's got to count for something. If you believed in the tooth fairy once, then you are capable of believing in yourself.

Not everything is going to help you to heal, but something will. You've got to try and to keep trying. I couldn't sit still and meditate after Ben died. I couldn't bear to be alone with my thoughts or to connect with my breath or body, because it was just another brutal reminder that Ben couldn't breathe, that he was no longer in his. Instead, my meditation comes in the form of lifting weights, being in nature, and dancing to my favourite music. The definition of meditation is to engage in mental exercise for the purpose of reaching a heightened level of awareness. I would assume, then, that we don't need to sit cross-legged, chanting mantras and fingering mala beads in order for something to constitute a meditative practice. We get to decide what our healing looks like. Stay open. It's possible to find it in places you'd least expect to.

Lastly, I hope that Ben's life and death inspires you to reach for joy. To pursue a life you truly love living, and to hold your loved ones closer. We always think we have more time until we don't. We think our people will be around forever, until they are not. I'm not really sure how we're supposed to reconcile with that. I don't think we can completely, because it's impossible to live every day like it's our last. Things get in the way, we sweat the small stuff. We have bills and rent and mortgage repayments due, we're tired after a busy week at work. But I think we can commit to loving each other a little harder. We can defy death with our films, our books, our music, our art. We can strive to live every day knowing that our time here, in this incarnation, is finite. The odds that we are even here in the first place are 1 in $10^{2,685,000}$. That's ten followed by two million, six hundred and eighty-five thousand zeros. We are miracles. Each of us, a temporary collaboration of atoms dancing together on a floating rock, or as astronomer Carl Sagan once put it, on a mote of dust suspended in a sunbeam. If that isn't enough of a reason to grab our life by the horns and make the best of it, I don't know what is.

1

You know the saying about having to kiss a lot of frogs before you find your prince? Well, *that*. Throughout my teens and early twenties, I managed to make some spectacularly bad decisions when it came to dating. I don't want to be that person who blames their parents for the way they turned out, but I have a feeling my dad might have had something to do with it.

I could tell you a lot about my mum, Angi. She grew up in the South Cotswolds village of Minchinhampton, and excelled in sports and science at school. She sold property all over London in the seventies. She speaks Greek, and loves to read non-fiction narratives that explore cultures radically different to her own, influencing my passion for languages and books at a young age. Her cooking is nothing short of culinary wizardry. She loves dirty jokes as much as I do, and her sense of the ridiculous always leaves me bent over double, clutching the sides of my ribcage and howling with laughter. She's my confidante, my cheerleader, my best friend, and we've always been really close.

As for my dad Steve? I couldn't tell you much about him, you know. It's not that he was a *bad* dad. Definitely not. I guess you could say he was a sort of 'there but not really' kind of dad. An emotionally unavailable, 'found it difficult to express love' dad. By the time I was fifteen, I went looking for male approval and affection elsewhere – elsewhere being the beer garden in the Wetherspoons pub on Tonbridge High Street, Kent.

It was the place to be – or so my friends and I thought. The pub itself wasn't exactly the classiest of joints, with sticky carpets and chronically blocked toilets, but back then, being underage and swindling the Serbian bouncer with a fake ID at the door, it was about as exciting as it got. I met my first boyfriend there a few weeks before my sixteenth birthday. We started going out a few months later, and spent the next year doing doughnuts in his Seat Ibiza in various car parks around town. When he turned up at our house for the first time wearing a gold chain and tight white tank top, reeking of Lynx Africa and cigarettes, my older brother Oliver could barely conceal his horror. After countless overly dramatic arguments about nothing, most of which ended with him on his knees begging for my forgiveness, I eventually saw sense and broke up with him. My stepdad Dougal had to give him a stern talking-to one evening, after finding him parked up outside our house, watching me through my bedroom window.

Several years and bad decisions later, I started dating an infantry soldier in the Parachute Regiment who I knew from my Wetherspoons era. It was 2012, and I'd just moved back into Mum and Dougal's house in Tonbridge after graduating from Nottingham University with a 2:1 in French Studies. After a heated discussion at his one night, I'd scurried off to the bathroom with his phone to scroll through his messages in secret. Granted, it's never a good idea to look through somebody's phone – technically, I *had* breached his privacy. But more to the point, he'd slept with not one but five girls while I was backpacking around South East Asia. I was only gone for four weeks – how did he even have the time for it? I was horrified and heartbroken, and yet somehow I was the one who ended up apologising. 'I'm sorry,' I sobbed, stuffing my toothbrush and knickers into my overnight bag as he marched me towards his front door. I promised never to look at his phone again. He slammed it shut and blocked my number, and I haven't heard from him since.

A few months after he broke things off, Mum and Dougal moved to Shropshire, a county in the West Midlands, in search of greener pastures. I'd just started a new job in Soho in London, working as an assistant at a post-production house on Wardour Street, and had decided to stay put. Plus, boyfriend number five had just appeared on the scene. I waved them off and moved into the spare bedroom at my dad's house in Tunbridge Wells instead. We hadn't lived together since I was fifteen. To live under the same roof, all these years later, would either make or break our relationship. To my pleasant surprise it made it, so much so that we established a few of our own father-daughter traditions. Friday nights became curry nights, which were typically spent arguing about climate change over piles of paneer tikka. On Saturdays, we'd sift through his vinyl collection and dance to The Doors or Amy Winehouse blasting from the vintage stereo in his living room. On Sundays, we'd head up the road to the yoga class at the community centre together. He'd turned my invitation to attend down at first. Yoga, he'd decided, was reserved for the smelly bohemian types who wore harem pants and only ate tofu and lentils. But when I eventually managed to convince him to come with me, he was practically skipping out of the studio door after class. He loved it, just as I knew he would. Every Sunday morning from that day forward, he'd insist on arriving ten minutes early to nab a spot at the front, donning the new pair of navy tracksuit bottoms he'd bought especially from the TK Maxx shop in town. The teacher would often use him for his demonstrations, which, given he was about as flexible as a steel girder, often showed the rest of us how *not* to do a pose. But I guess it was the effort that counted.

'They can't *all* be bad,' I said to Chloe. It was the August bank holiday weekend in 2014, and we were sitting outside a bar overlooking Regent's Canal in east London, scrolling through a list of possible candidates on one of the latest dating apps. My best friend since we were eleven, she'd heard her fair share of the boyfriend horror stories over the years. I was in my rebound phase, having dumped number five six months earlier. His proclivity for weekend benders had finally got between us, and I'd moved out of the spare room at Dad's in Kent into a flat in Clapham, south-west London, in pursuit of a fresh start. All I wanted was a distraction, a snog, perhaps – but so far my search hadn't yielded any fruit. The small talk that was part and parcel of online dating was rarely interesting enough for me to make it to phase two – an actual date.

'You'll meet the right person when you least expect to,' she said, taking a sip of her Aperol spritz. She'd met her boyfriend Mark the month before on a night out in Peckham. He was lucky snog number three, and the first bloke she'd ever asked to go home with her the same night she'd met him. He'd politely declined, and offered to take her out for dinner the following week instead. 'That's when I knew he was a keeper,' she sniggered, her long brown hair tumbling over her shoulders.

'Oh my God,' I gasped suddenly, grabbing her arm. 'Take a look at *him*.' I turned my phone towards her so she could see what I was seeing. The boy in question was called Ben. He was thirty years old, a music agent, and utterly gorgeous – the 'stop you in your tracks and make your head turn twice' kind of gorgeous – with a spectacular tan, curly brown hair, just the right amount of beard, and green eyes. I'd be lying if I said I didn't have a type. Ben was it: dark hair, dark skin. But more than that – he looked kind. It was something about his eyes. They stirred something in me, the way they stared into the lens, open and clear and vulnerable. But could I really draw conclusions about somebody based on a few photos?

I glanced at Chloe, who gave me a knowing look – chin dropped, one eyebrow raised, her lips curling upwards in a mischievous smile. It was a look I'd come to know well over the years. We'd been joined at the hip ever since the first day of German class at secondary school. She was smart but gloriously naughty like me, and we'd bonded over our shared love of cracking jokes and misbehaving when the teacher wasn't looking. We soon developed an uncanny way of sensing what the other was thinking or feeling without the need for words. There wasn't so much an inner circle to us, more an inner line that went straight from me to her, to me again. She gave me a nod and I swiped right, and a burst of confetti appeared on my screen. I felt a hint of dopamine sparkle in my veins that often came with the validation of a handsome stranger. He had already beat me to it.

'I'm going to wait for him to message me first,' I told Chloe. I slipped my phone into my bag and we headed back to the bar for another drink.

As I turned the key in the lock of my front door a few hours later, my phone flashed up with a notification. It was a message from Ben.

'Hello Lotte!' the message read. 'How are you doing?'

I stepped inside the hallway and pulled my shoes off, wondering whether to text him back or not. If I texted him too soon I'd probably come across as too keen. If I left it for a while, he might lose interest. My thumbs hovered over the keypad as I wandered into my bedroom and flicked on the light.

'Hi Ben! Nice to meet you,' I wrote, climbing out of my jeans. *No*, I thought. It wasn't smart or witty or flirty enough. I deleted it, wrote another message, and deleted that one too. *Oh, fuck it.* I pulled my pyjamas on and checked the time. It was almost three o'clock in the morning. A reply would have to wait until the three glasses of vodka and cranberry juice were no longer chugging through my bloodstream and I was a tad more compos mentis. I threw my phone onto my bedside table, collapsed into bed and fell fast asleep.

Several hours later, I woke to my housemates banging pots and slamming drawers in the kitchen next door. Rubbing the sleep from my eyes, I rolled over and reached for my phone.

'Good morning Ben!' I typed. 'I'm good, thank you, how are you?' It was neither smart, nor witty nor flirty – but why should it have been? *He'd only asked me how I was*, for Christ's sake. What was the use in overthinking it, in playing games? I clambered out of bed and reached for my dressing gown hanging on the back of the door when my phone pinged.

'I'm good too, thanks! How's your day going so far?'

Wow, I thought. *Speedy.*

I lay sprawled on the sofa for the afternoon texting him, only coming up for air to examine the contents of the fridge for snacks. The small talk that usually left me feeling underwhelmed or bored, or both, only made me more curious. He told me that he lived in Clapton in east London. He'd studied music technology at Derby University, and had just joined The Agency Group as a fully fledged music agent after climbing the ranks from booking assistant at another smaller agency over the last few years.

I couldn't pretend that I wasn't impressed. I was passionate about music too, ever since I'd picked up a violin at a family friend's house one afternoon when I was nine years old. I'd watched, mesmerised, as one of the older children struck the bow against the strings and played Edvard Grieg's 'Hall of the Mountain King'. Tracing my fingers along the horse hair that ran between the ends of the bow, I decided there and then that I wanted to learn how to play it too. My mum was thrilled, and booked me a lesson for after school the following week. She could tell that the violin had sparked a love for classical music, and soon after, bought a digital piano to add to our growing repertoire of instruments at home. I would pore over the theory books she bought me for hours on end, learning different scales, chords, and arpeggios. I'd listen to songs on repeat, like Ludovico Einaudi's 'Le Onde' and Beethoven's 'Für Elise', reproducing a rudimentary version of my own that I'd perform for her once I'd deemed it good enough for an audience. Growing up in the sixties and seventies, Mum had fabulous taste in music. Soul, Motown, folk and pop echoed through our house most evenings after she arrived home from work. We would twirl around the kitchen with my big sister Georgia, the three of us singing into spatulas and drumming our knuckles against the pots and pans.

Years later, a defining moment on a packed-out dance floor in south London had marked the beginning of my love affair with dance music. The DJ Carl Cox played a remix of 'The Man with the Red Face' in the dance tent at South West Four festival on Clapham Common. I turned to Georgia dancing next to me, wide-eyed with delight, as the syrupy sound of the saxophone swept through my body.

Ben, it turned out, had been there too. 'I'd have definitely remembered you though if I'd seen you,' he wrote.

'Me too,' I replied, grinning. I glanced towards the living room door that led onto the patio outside. I was so engrossed in our conversation I'd barely noticed it getting dark. I peeled myself off the sofa and wandered towards the bathroom, yawning.

'I should probably go to sleep now,' I texted him as I stood leaning over the sink, brushing my teeth.

'I should too,' he replied. 'Although all I want to do is talk to you.'

'The feeling's mutual. Let's pick up where we left off tomorrow. I'll message you in the morning.' I sent him a kiss, and left my phone face down on the bedside table, willing myself not to check to see if he'd replied until the following morning.

The next day, the conversation between us showed no signs of slowing down. I sat at my desk in Ladbroke Grove, west London, my phone glued to my hand. I needed to put it away, to focus on the sales calls I'd been postponing all morning. If you'd asked me what my dream career was, selling advertising space on a wellness influencer's WordPress blog was definitely not it, but I'd just left my job at the post-production house in Soho and was feeling a little lost. I had high hopes when I started working for her. I'd discovered a love for all things health and fitness, having qualified as a yoga teacher at the community centre back in Kent before I moved out of Dad's house, and loved to spend hours in the kitchen poring over new recipes – but so far, the reality of the job left much to be desired. She would breathe down my neck, her beady eyes glued to the tabs I had open on my laptop to make sure every available minute was spent working. During my lunch breaks, she'd corner me in the kitchen to bitch about other bloggers. I'd sit there, nodding quietly, hoping she'd get the hint and leave me to eat my food in peace. Luckily, she was out of the office today and not due back until gone four o'clock. Our conversation could slip by unnoticed.

Hours later at half past five, I slammed the lid of my laptop and pulled my bag out from underneath the desk. 'Have you actually done any work?' I texted him.

'Nope,' he answered. 'All I've done is send you songs.'

I'd listened to all of the songs he had sent me that afternoon. There wasn't a single one I didn't love, but the first song was my favourite. It was called 'Nukumori', produced by one of his clients, an artist called Simon Stokes who went by the name of Petrichor. I looked up the meaning of the song title on my phone as I wandered between the stalls in Portobello Road market towards Ladbroke Grove station. Nukumori was a Japanese word used to describe a kind of palpable warmth – the presence of a person not dependent on physical proximity, that stays with you even if they can't. I smiled to myself as I passed through the ticket barrier at the station entrance. Ben was certainly beginning to preoccupy my thoughts, and I liked him there. I untangled the string of headphones from my jacket pocket and pressed 'Play' again as I boarded the next train back to Clapham. The *tsss tsss* of the hi-hat started, punctured by claps, with warm, gooey synths building and building. I wormed my way towards an empty seat at the far end of the carriage and sat down. 'I believe that love,' came a voice, 'is an eternal power.'[1] The melody was mesmerising. I closed my eyes and let it lift me out of the carriage, up through the ground over London and into the clouds. If there was ever a song that sounded like falling in love, I thought, this was it.

The next evening, I was standing at the kitchen counter making dinner – tagliatelle with red onion, sun-dried tomatoes, spinach, basil and feta, when up popped his name on my phone.

'Shall we run off to Berlin one weekend?' his message read. 'The nightlife is meant to be incredible.'

'When are we going?' I replied, biting into a ribbon of undercooked pasta. It was odd – making future plans with a man I'd yet to meet in person felt like the most normal thing in the world. Given my track record, I probably ought to have exercised some caution, held back a bit. He was, after all, a relative stranger that I didn't know existed until a few days ago. I pushed the vegetables around as they sautéed in the pan, my phone still glued to my other hand.

---

1   Lyrics taken from 'Nukumori' by Petrichor (Soma Records), with thanks to Simon Stokes.

'That would be the best date ever,' he replied. 'Meeting at the airport – provided you're not catfishing me, of course.'

'Speaking of dates . . .' I paused for a moment. 'When are you going to ask me out?' I dragged in a sharp breath and stared at the ellipsis next to his name, oblivious to the vegetables burning on the bottom of the pan.

'Well,' he wrote. 'I'm free next Thursday?'

Butterflies fluttered inside my chest at the mere thought of it. But what if this virtual connection didn't translate face to face? Maybe I'd built him up to be something that he wasn't, maybe it wouldn't be as good as I'd imagined it to be. But then again, what if it *was* as good? What if it was even better, in fact? I checked my Google calendar – nothing.

'Me too,' I texted back. 'Let's do it.'

'How about Shoreditch House for dinner? I'll make a reservation. Say 7 p.m.?'

First dates usually only warranted a drink. A drink was casual, non-committal. It gave you a chance to feel into things a bit, and to plot an escape route if you wanted out. But he wanted to skip forwards a step, to sit across from me at a fancy members' club, watching me *eat*. Well, so did I actually. Judging by how much we'd spoken over the last seventy-two hours, how effortless it had been between us, it made sense to keep moving at the pace we'd started with. And I wanted nothing more than to find a quiet corner of Shoreditch where I could get lost in him for hours on end.

'Great,' I said. 'It's a date.'

2

Thursday couldn't come round soon enough. I emerged above ground at Liverpool Street station after work, and made my way through the crowds towards Brushfield Street. It was an unusually warm evening for September. The burnt orange sun reflected off the glass office blocks that stood tall among rows of Georgian townhouses. I checked my watch. It was six o'clock, which meant I had an hour to spare – just enough time to make use of the testers at MAC in Spitalfields Market. Running for nearly three hundred and fifty years, it's one of London's oldest markets, now home to dozens of artisanal food stalls and trendy clothes shops. I pushed through the doors of the shop and made a beeline for some bronzer to dust my cheeks with. I applied some concealer and lipstick, and examined my choice of outfit in the mirror: a white t-shirt, now with very visible sweat patches, faded blue jeans and black boots.

Hmm, I thought to myself. *No. This won't do.* I needed something different – something without the sweat patches, first and foremost. I sifted through the rails in the clothes shop next door and landed on another white t-shirt and black faux-leather mini skirt. I handed the money to the girl behind the checkout, got changed, and joined the stream of shoppers spilling onto the street outside. As I passed under the railway bridge on Braithwaite Street,

I spotted him in the distance. He was standing opposite the station entrance, dressed in a loose grey t-shirt and black jeans.

'Oh my God,' I uttered under my breath as I walked towards him. He was even more handsome in real life. I caught sight of myself in a car window and readjusted my skirt when he turned in my direction.

'There you are! How are you doing?' He threw his arm around me and kissed me on the cheek.

'I'm great, thank you,' I replied, reeling from the sensation of his hand on my back. 'It's nice to actually meet you in person. It's weird, I feel like I already know you?'

'Same,' he laughed, revealing a brilliant, toothy smile.

We crossed the road towards Shoreditch House on the corner of Ebor Street. After signing our names in at reception, we stepped inside the lift. I caught the scent of the cologne on his neck as he leaned past me to press the button for the sixth floor – notes of spice and sandalwood. *Delicious.* I wanted him to stay close to me for a moment so I could savour the smell. A handful of people entered the lift as we climbed higher, sandwiching us closer together. He looked at me, registered my features. My cheeks flushed hot as I suddenly became very aware of myself. What was he thinking? Did he like what he saw?

'Ladies first,' he said, gesturing for me to step outside as the doors opened. I stepped out onto the rooftop to rows of sunbeds surrounding an open-air swimming pool, set against a backdrop of skyscrapers in the distance. He led me past the pool towards the entrance of the restaurant, where a pretty hostess with cropped black hair greeted us from behind the stand.

'Welcome,' she said, smiling. She handed us each a menu, and showed us to a table in the far corner of the restaurant. 'What would you like to drink?' Her presence served as a buffer, a moment for me to catch my breath as we sat down.

'Just water for now?' Ben looked at me. I nodded.

I traced the constellation of freckles on his perfect, aquiline nose, set between thick eyelashes as he studied the menu. His looks, I noticed, ought to have intimidated me. In my experience, men this devilishly handsome usually had an air of arrogance, an 'I can do whatever the fuck I want' attitude without caring what the consequences were. But something about him told me that he was different. Maybe it was the way he carried himself, the way he'd failed to notice the many eyes that had followed him through the restaurant as we headed to our table.

A lithe, blonde-haired waiter soon appeared beside us with a bottle of sparkling water and a bowl of kalamata olives.

'Cheers,' said Ben, grinning at me, glass in hand.

I smiled back at him. *There it is again*, I thought to myself. That brilliant, toothy smile.

The next few hours passed by unnoticed as we talked and talked over crudités, whipped burrata and margherita pizza. I learned that he was one of nine children, seven of whom were half-siblings. He'd moved to Malaga on the southern coast of Spain when he was eight years old, and could speak Spanish fluently. His mum and dad, Jean and Clem, had decided to relocate to the Costa Del Sol in 1992 just before Clem retired. Growing up, summers were spent wakeboarding in Estepona, and winters snowboarding in Andalucia. Christiaan, his older brother, lived in Nottingham with his girlfriend Nicole. Ben and Christiaan shared a love of music, DJing at all the local pubs and clubs around Marbella in their teens.

As I took the last few bites of my pizza, we retraced our steps around London over the summer. We'd been to the same places and the same club nights, weaving in and out of each other's worlds without ever actually crossing paths. 'I'd have definitely remembered you,' he'd said to me yesterday, his words echoing in my mind still. But it was strange – I did remember him somehow. He felt familiar to me, as if I recognised his soul from someplace else.

At half past eleven, the waiter who'd taken our orders returned to our table to bring us the bill unprompted. *Not now*, I thought. I wanted more of him. Other diners had come and gone and neither of us had noticed. We could've been the only two people in the restaurant for all I cared. We paid the bill and headed back into the lift and out onto Ebor Street, before heading south towards Liverpool Street station to catch the last trains home. The air was still thick with heat, the streets heaving. We passed through the ticket barrier at the station and turned towards each other to say our goodbyes. I stole a glance at his lips, wondering what it would feel like to kiss them. I wanted to, and badly – but not here, not in front of all these strangers. Our first kiss deserved more than that. He leaned forwards and kissed me on the cheek, the feel of his lips still lingering on my skin as he pulled away.

He disappeared round the corner to catch the overground back to Clapton, and I descended the stairs towards the Tube, my body still tingling with the feeling of him up against me.

When the train pulled into Clapham Common station, I climbed the stairs and pulled my phone from my pocket. His name flashed up. 'I had so much fun this evening,' he wrote. 'Let's do it again asap?'

'You read my mind,' I typed as I walked along the path that cut through the common, a smile spreading across my face like a Cheshire cat's.

◆ ◆ ◆

We planned to meet up again a couple of days later beneath the billboards at the entrance to the O2 Arena on the Greenwich Peninsula, south-east London. One of his artists, a Dutch DJ who went by the name of Ferreck Dawn, was warming up for Kylie Minogue on her Kiss Me Once tour. We picked up our passes at the box office inside the entrance and headed past security through a labyrinth of corridors backstage. It felt surreal. Every superstar act I'd grown up listening to, from Beyoncé to Prince to the Rolling Stones, had taken these very steps. We stopped occasionally to study the countless gold and platinum record plaques hanging on the walls. This was some second date, I thought. He looked at me and winked, as if having read my mind. Another security check, another laminated pass. We continued along the corridor and the music grew louder, the bass line rebounding off the walls. *We're not actually going onstage, are we?* I wondered. *Shit.* At the very most, I'd hoped to catch the show from the wings, out of sight. We passed through a web of curtains and headed towards a flight of stairs.

'Come on,' said Ben, holding out his hand.

We climbed the stairs, two at a time, and stepped out under the bright white lights onto the stage. I stood there for a moment to take it in, gawping. I'd watched so many concerts here over the years, but to see the vastness of this space, from this vantage point, was something else. Who *was* this man? I needed to find out.

A couple of hours later, once the show had finished, we jumped in a black cab and headed back to Clapham.

'I'd never usually do this,' I told him as we drove past Dulwich Park. I'd never invited a man home with me as early as two dates in. But then, this didn't feel like the second date. It felt like we'd had dozens of them before – hundreds, even.

'I must be special then,' he grinned.

The taxi pulled up outside my front door and we tiptoed inside. I showed him into my room and he sat on my bed as I pulled my pyjamas on, the energy between us electric.

'Why does it feel so good to be close to you?' he asked as we climbed into bed.

'I don't know,' I laughed.

He pulled me closer to him. 'I haven't felt anything like this before, you know.' His voice faltered, as if the admission had just stripped him bare, revealing his vulnerability.

My stomach flipped. I hadn't either. I pressed my palm against his cheek, his face illuminated by the sliver of moonlight spilling through the curtains. He leaned towards me and our lips met in a slow, lingering kiss. This was the start of something significant, I thought, as I melted into his arms. It had to be. I didn't know how or what it might look like, but I was sure this man would change my life.

3

A few weeks later, we were walking hand in hand back to my flat after work.

'You should come,' he insisted. He was due to fly to the Netherlands in a fortnight's time for Amsterdam Dance Event, an electronic music conference and festival that took over different clubs, warehouses, hotels and record stores throughout the city every October. His schedule would be busy with meetings and shows, but we could meet up in-between. 'You could even come to some of the shows if you wanted to,' he offered.

'Hmm,' I replied, mulling over his invitation. Would I really follow him to another country, just a few weeks in to dating? *Yes,* I thought. *I would.* I would probably follow him to the other side of the world, given the chance. By normal standards, things were moving quickly between us – maybe even too quickly – but who wanted normal? I knew I certainly didn't. This, I was beginning to realise, was what had been missing from my life. Excitement, spontaneity. Adventure. It was not that it was bad before, it was just that it felt, well, lacking. Like there was more to be felt and experienced.

When we pushed through my front door and kicked off our shoes, I pulled my phone from my bag and texted my friend Annie. 'Do you fancy coming to Amsterdam with me next month?'

Annie and her boyfriend Will had been in the year below me at university. She lived twenty minutes away in Tulse Hill and had just joined the same yoga studio as me by the common. We'd sometimes meet up for a class and a juice before work.

'Oh my God, yes!' she replied instantly. 'I'd love to. When are you thinking?'

◆ ◆ ◆

On a Thursday evening in mid-October, Annie and I were sitting beside the window of a cosy, candlelit restaurant overlooking one of Amsterdam's many canals. 'How are you feeling about Ben?' she quizzed over the sound of soft chatter and cutlery clinking against porcelain.

'Excited,' I gushed, pushing my food around my plate. 'Kind of nervous . . . I don't know. He's amazing, Annie. I think I might be falling for him.' Except I didn't just think it – I knew it. It sounded completely absurd. Was it even possible to fall for somebody this quickly? In the grand scheme of things, we barely knew each other. It defied all logic, but it felt so natural, so right at the same time.

'I don't doubt it,' she exclaimed, revealing a set of perfect teeth. 'I'm so excited *for* you!'

I smiled at her. Everybody needed an Annie in their lives, I thought. In a short space of time she'd become like a sister to me – a true ally in every sense of the word. She continually rooted for my happiness. And I didn't have to worry about her feeling like a third wheel – she was a big romantic, and loved love.

We hurried through the rest of dinner, paid up, pulled on our coats and stepped outside. I gasped as the cold night air whipped against my skin. Linking arms for extra warmth, we dashed along the cobblestone pathway towards the nearest taxi rank, the canal next to us shimmering with the soft glow of street lamps. We climbed into the back of the car, relieved to enter the warmth again, and drove north to a club on the harbourfront where Ben had told us to meet him. He was standing outside the venue as the car pulled up to the kerb.

'Hi, girls,' he beamed as we clambered out. We hugged each other tightly. There they were again – those butterflies in my chest. The three of us pushed our way through the partygoers pouring onto the pavement and headed past security towards the main room inside. Thousands of people stood coiled tightly together on the dance floor, their bodies swaying, arms skyward. A kaleidoscope of colours swirled overhead in time with the undulating bass. It reverberated through my arms and legs and into my feet, making the hairs on the back of my neck stand on end.

'What do you want to drink?' Ben shouted over the music.

'A vodka lime and soda?' I suggested.

Annie nodded.

'Great! I fancy one too – I'll meet you back here in a minute.'

He disappeared into the queue, emerging a few minutes later with three drinks in hand.

'Let's dance, shall we?' he said, signalling for us to head into the crowd. Over the six weeks we had known each other, I'd learned that, like me, he didn't like to loiter on the periphery of the action. The closer, the better. We squeezed our way through the horde of sweat-slicked brows and flushed faces to the middle of the dance floor. I felt his fingertips suddenly brush against the small of my back, the gesture just enough to send a shiver up my spine. They remained glued there as I swayed and looped my hips.

'Excuse me.' A man dancing next to us tapped Ben on the shoulder. 'Is this your girlfriend?' he asked, nodding in my direction.

'Um . . .' Ben laughed nervously. 'I don't know – *are* you my girlfriend, Lotte?'

I looked at Annie, who winked at me, her eyes sparkling with enthusiasm.

'I mean . . , Yeah! I guess so?' I laughed and kissed him on the mouth, dragging my thumbs over his lips to wipe off the stain my lipstick had left behind.

'You guys!' Annie cheered, clapping her hands together. 'I'm so happy I just got to witness that. What an honour.'

The three of us hugged and headed closer to the stage. I watched as others orbited him. I understood the pull. He radiated good energy, the sort you wanted to be around and that made you feel good in return. *He's with me*, I thought, as he gave each person a dazzling smile and the undivided attention of his arresting eyes. *That incredible man could have chosen anyone, and he chose me.* I felt like the luckiest girl in the world.

A couple of days later, I kissed Annie goodbye outside of our hotel as she climbed into the back of a taxi headed for the airport. I flagged down another and travelled across town to Ben's hotel in De Pijp, Amsterdam's Latin Quarter. The car pulled up outside a beautiful Baroque-style canal house with a gabled facade. As I stepped inside, my eyes took a moment to adjust to the riot of colour in front of me. The foyer, lined with tropical plants, was painted cobalt blue. I glanced around to find Ben sitting on one of the tinsel-red modular ball chairs clustered together in the far corner. His face lit up as our eyes met.

'Hi.' He stood up and waved. 'You look gorgeous!'

I felt a rush of blood to my cheeks as I walked over to him. 'Thanks, babe.' I smiled and kissed him on the lips. 'So do you.'

'Shall we head upstairs and drop off your stuff?'

He closed the lid of his laptop and, ever the gentleman, insisted he carry my bag for me. I followed him up the narrow spiral staircase and into the room we would be sharing for the next couple of nights. Chintzy wallpaper clashed against bright magenta curtains. The canopy bed, draped in layers of velvet, stood like a regal centrepiece amidst all the chaos.

'Where did you find this place?' I asked him.

He grinned at me and shrugged. 'I know. I left it to the last minute to book somewhere.'

We set my bag down and grabbed our jackets before heading back outside in the direction of the Albert Cuyp market. Baskets of fresh fruit, vibrant spices, cheese and chocolate stood next to flower stalls, rails of vintage clothes and tables covered in knick-knacks. Wafts of raw herring and *stroopwafels* mingled in the air as we weaved our way through the thoroughfare, pausing occasionally to sift through crates of vinyl and sample cubes of Dutch Gouda on cocktail sticks. Just beyond the far end of the market was a Dutch smart shop with a large red mushroom sign hanging above the door. A smart shop, Ben had explained, was a purveyor of psychoactive substances. Along with your usual pick 'n' mix of cannabis, magic truffles, mushrooms, peyote and San Pedro cactus, you could buy all kinds of weird and wonderful paraphernalia, like dick-shaped bongs and crystals the guy behind the till will insist heal your back-ache.

'Shall we take a look inside?' Ben suggested. He pushed open the door and we wandered in to be greeted by a thickset man sitting behind the till, fingering an assortment of tarnished silver necklaces resting on top of his belly. Shelves stacked high with small colourful boxes lined the aisles. Stood next to them were crystals in different colours, shapes and sizes, each with a laminated plaque beside them with detailed descriptions of their healing properties.

'What sort of truffles would you suggest taking for your first trip?' Ben turned and asked the man.

'Hmm,' he uttered, stepping out from behind the counter. 'Let me see.' He traced a stubby finger along one of the shelves. 'Bingo! These ones are my favourite.' He pulled a box down and handed it to Ben. It had a blue label on it that read, 'Atlantis: Forbidden Fruit. Read the label before use.' 'If this is your first foray into psychedelics,' he continued, 'a box between the two of you will be plenty.' Ben and I looked at each other. He had a glint in his eyes that said, 'Fancy it?'

I thought about it for a moment. I'd never considered myself religious, but I'd always been curious. When I was younger, I went to a Church of England primary school. My parents weren't religious either, but it was one of the few schools with a decent reputation in the area. Every morning, we'd pile into the main hall for assembly to sing Bible songs like 'He's Got the Whole World in His Hands' and 'Give Me Oil in My Lamp'. We'd celebrate the harvest festival in October, taking cardboard boxes filled with canned food to the nearby church to be handed out to local hospitals and charities. And that was really about as far as it went. The idea of a bearded man behind gilded gates in the sky who decided everyone's fate just didn't wash with me – but still, I felt there had to be something more, something beyond the limited scope of my senses. How arrogant to assume that this was all there was? Maybe now was the time to find out. And who better to explore it with, than Ben?

'I'm up for it if you are,' I answered. 'Let's just do the one box, though, yeah?' Better to take the man's advice and dip a toe in the water. We could always eat more, but we couldn't eat less.

Ben handed the man a crisp twenty-euro note from his pocket.

'*Bedankt!*' The man smiled. He stuffed the note into the till drawer and slammed it shut. 'You're in for a fun afternoon.' He winked at us and waved us out of the door.

We hurried back to our hotel, arm in arm, and climbed the winding staircase.

'What do you think we should do?' I asked him, kicking my trainers off as I jumped onto the bed. He retrieved the box of truffles from my bag and sat down next to me.

'I reckon we eat them here, wait for them to kick in, and then go and explore.' He prised open the box and separated the truffles into two portions. 'This is for you.' He passed me a handful. I rolled them over in my hand and examined them. They looked like the sort of truffles you'd shave onto a pasta dish – brown and bumpy on the outside, only much more yellow, as if they'd long passed their sell-by date. '*Bon appétit!*'

'Bottoms up,' I replied, taking a deep breath and knocking a few back. 'UGH!' I coughed, my face contorted with disgust. 'Christ!' The taste was astonishing – what I'd imagine a cocktail of soil, rotten fruit and cow shit to taste like. I forced down another and retched. 'Quick,' I said to Ben, pointing to the bottle of water on his bedside table. I pinched my nose and swallowed them quickly with some water, hoping it might dilute the taste of shit now lingering in my mouth.

We pulled back the duvet and slid into bed together. Twenty minutes passed and nothing happened, except for the occasional stomach gripe. *Oh God, not now*, I thought. The last thing I needed was to end up legs akimbo on the toilet next door with the squits, with only a paper-thin wall between us. I looked around the room in search of a sign, the air crackling with anticipation.

'It takes time,' Ben reminded me, laughing. 'Be patient.'

I swung my legs round to the edge of the bed and lifted myself to my feet.

'Whoa!' I steadied myself against the bedside table. Something was definitely beginning to happen, although I wasn't quite sure what exactly. I ran my fingers along the underwire of my bra, my clothes feeling restrictive all of a sudden. I wanted to feel free, more limber to move around. I pulled a t-shirt and tracksuit bottoms out of my bag and got changed.

Ben wandered over to the radio on top of the chest of drawers with his phone in his hand. 'We need a soundtrack for this, don't we?' He fiddled with the buttons on the radio for a moment. *Beep.* Music started streaming from the speakers, a soft and steady bassline filling the room.

Yawning, I climbed back into bed and closed my eyes.

'Breathe,' I told myself, tracing my hands over my belly and chest. In. And out. The guitar lick poured down my throat, thick and warm like honey. After some time, colours started dancing across my eyelids. *Dum de de dum.* Pink. Orange. *Dum de de dum.* Yellow. I felt as though I was floating, weightless. Untethered. Ben's hands found their way to me, and he pulled me into him. I melted into his chest, the boundaries between us blurring. *Where does he end, and I begin?* I wondered. I couldn't be sure. His chest rose and fell in time with mine.

'How are you feeling?' he asked, his lips brushing against my forehead.

'Mmm,' I murmured. 'Delicious.' The music chugged slowly and deliberately through my veins, coalescing with the truffles and pulling me deeper. I drifted in and out of focus, lingering at the threshold of what felt like a different realm. I'd read that, like magic mushrooms, magic truffles contained the psychedelic compound psilocybin, which can cause changes in perception, hallucinations, feelings of euphoria, and perceived mystical experiences. This was mystical alright, I thought to myself. Did I even *have* a body anymore? Who knew. It was as if I were being stripped of all my bodily binding. Every exhalation pulled me under even further. Who was I *really*? I found myself wondering. Was I the role I played as a daughter, a sister, a partner, a friend? Was I my job, or the hobbies

I had at weekends? Was I the thoughts I had, the things I did? Was I flesh and bone? No. I was more than that. I wasn't my body, I was none of those things. Rather, I was a soul. A slice of the Divine, expressing itself for a while in human form. The Aztecs were said to have heralded the mushroom as 'the flesh of the gods', and for good reason. The truffles stirred a quiet sense of something bigger, something far greater than my mind could fully comprehend. A higher intelligence *did* exist – a kind of love that suffused everything. This intelligence was not separate from me. Rather, it was inside of me. It *was* me.

'I think so too,' Ben answered softly, as I shared my newfound insights with him. 'And I think . . .' He stalled for a second. I turned to look at him, his eyes closed and his eyebrows pulled together, deep in thought. 'I think we've been together before.'

Of course we had. It made perfect sense. I'd known it from the moment I'd caught sight of him two months ago, standing outside Shoreditch High Street station. He'd felt like home to me. As if we'd been together in different incarnations, and unseen forces had made our paths collide again. The past, present, and future versions of us, converging into a swirling, infinite now. All I'd wanted to say to him was, '*There* you are. What took you so long to find me?'

4

The cold night air was seeping through the living room walls. I pulled the wool blanket over my shoulders and huddled against Ben as we sunk deeper into my sofa. It was Halloween, and the *Ghostbusters* theme song thudded through the ceiling, punctuated by the click-clacking of high heels across the floorboards.

'Babe, there's something I've been wanting to tell you.'

'Oh yeah? What is it?'

'Well, I . . . I . . .' he stammered. 'I think I love you.'

A rush of oxytocin flooded my body as his words hung in the air.

'What did you just say?' I'd heard it perfectly the first time, but I wanted to hear it again.

'I love you,' he repeated, his voice more resolute this time.

'I love you too.' The words had wanted to spill from my mouth for weeks, the feeling now unquestionable. Our time in Amsterdam together two weekends before, tangled up in each other's limbs, our edges melding, had left no room for any doubt. I loved this man *completely*. I was built to love him – hell, I loved his bones. It's not like he made it hard for me though. There was very little not to love about him. Some people just have that special something that you can't quite put your finger on. Whatever it was, Ben had it in spades. If you could somehow architect the perfect human, I was certain he would have come close.

He kissed the top of my head and we sat there in silence for a while, marinating in those three words.

Love, or so I'd learned in the past, always came with certain conditions. The conditions usually went something along the lines of, 'Do less of this and be more of that, and *then* I'll love you.' In other words, don't be yourself, because you're not worthy enough as you are. Instead, mould yourself into who you think they want you to be. Love meant arguing, and arguing often. It was *healthy* to argue, or at least that was what I'd been told. It meant second-guessing the things you said and did. It meant ditching the skirts and dresses that might give other blokes 'the wrong impression'. It meant tolerating hurtful words because you'd stepped out of line, or even more hurtful hands.

But *this* love? This love was entirely different. *Ben* was different. He was kind and gentle and patient with me. We didn't argue, things didn't get out of hand. He didn't tell me what I could and couldn't wear. He lifted me up, empowered me. I didn't have to hide the parts of me that I considered less desirable. Every morning he'd insist that I looked beautiful, even though my eyes were puffy and last night's mascara had migrated south. I could just be myself, in all my messy, imperfect humanness. He loved me in the way that I'd longed to be loved. It was the kind of love I'd watched unfolding in all the Hollywood romcoms that ended with a happily ever after. I'd laid bare all of my insecurities, my foibles, my morning breath – and he hadn't run away.

It turns out that love wasn't actually supposed to make you feel crazy. It wasn't supposed to hurt that much. It wasn't meant to squash your self-esteem to within a mere inch of itself. You weren't meant to contort yourself into a version of what you thought you ought to be. And you needn't be fully healed either. The right person would tend to your broken parts, help you put them back together again. They would knock down the walls you built around your heart, and they would love every part of you – even the parts you tried so hard to keep hidden, the parts you deemed unlovable in the eyes of somebody else.

The following morning, I shuffled into the kitchen in my dressing gown to find him standing at the counter making breakfast. I walked up behind him and nestled into the warm curve of his neck.

'Coffee?' he asked.

'Yes, please.'

He poured the coffee from the cafetière and handed it to me, before spinning back round to attend to the baked beans bubbling on top of the hob. I pulled myself up onto the kitchen counter and watched as he cracked a box of eggs against the frying pan, the delicate shells coming apart between his fingers. I noticed the way he glided about between the pans, the toaster, the drawers – a sense of ease and grace in every step. He managed to make even the most mundane moments feel magical, I thought to myself. He was a thing of fascination to me – an exotic creature from some faraway land that I could have watched for hours on end.

'Hey, I was thinking . . .' He turned to me, one hand on his hip, spatula in the other. 'It makes sense for us to move in together soon, don't you think?'

I tugged at the corners of his t-shirt and pulled him towards me. 'It does, my love.' I smiled as I knotted my legs around his waist. 'We'd save on rent – *and* we wouldn't be caught off-guard with no clean undies.' I'd had to turn my knickers inside out after impromptu sleepovers more times than I could count.

He threw his head back and laughed. 'Exactly. We're together five nights out of seven anyway, and . . . I just want to be with you all the time.'

I felt the same. Five nights out of seven just wasn't cutting it. I wanted more of him, of us. He gave his notice to his landlord the next morning and, four weeks later, Georgia drove us both down to Clapham in her car with a dozen or so bags and boxes in the boot. I made some space in my wardrobe and chest of drawers for him, clearing out all the clothes I didn't want anymore to take to the charity shop on the high street. He chose the side of the bed he wanted to sleep on. He hung his dressing gown on the back of the bathroom door and popped his toothbrush in the glass by the sink next to mine. And that was it: we were living together. The beginning of Team Botty. It wasn't quite as sexy as Brangelina, but it was only right that we named our union.

The next few months passed us by in a whirlwind of technicolour. We became inseparable, two halves of one whole – only pulled apart when other things demanded our attention, like work and family and friends. We invented our own language, had our own private jokes – Bottyisms, they were called. When I wasn't with him, I was thinking about him. I seemed to miss him even when I *was* with him. My thirst couldn't be quenched, my appetite insatiable. Whether it was a hand on a thigh while making the morning commute on the Northern line together, or one foot on top of the other under the dinner table at night, we always had to be touching. Connected somehow. My body would fizz, as if his was a power bank that charged my cells.

By the time summer came, we danced our way across Europe, every other weekend spent at another festival or on another dance floor abroad. We ventured to Glastonbury Festival in the heart of Somerset in England, to Slottsfjell Festival in the oldest city in Norway, nested between giant, majestic fjords. We danced behind the DJ booth at Ambasada Gavioli nightclub in Slovenia, and at the iconic Pikes hotel in Ibiza. It was the stuff of my wildest dreams – the sort of things I'd read about in magazines, only now I was actually living them, with the man I was sure was the love of my life. I couldn't believe my luck. Unbridled joy found a home in every atom of my being. Falling in love with him felt like stepping through a hidden door into another world where colours existed that I hadn't seen before. My life, it seemed, was only just beginning to come into focus. I couldn't remember what it had been like before, let alone imagine ever living without him now.

Over the next few years, Ben's career as a music agent continued to flourish. He grew an impressive roster of clients, including Australian songwriter and producer Hayden James, Dominican-American Grammy award-winning DJ and producer Roger Sanchez, and Craig David, one of England's best loved garage and R & B artists from the nineties and noughties, whose pop career Ben was instrumental in reviving. After surviving on baked beans and beer in his teens and twenties, and sleeping in pop-up tents barely big enough to fit a small child inside, he was spending his festival days backstage rubbing shoulders with the likes of Kate Moss and Dave Grohl, booking slots on some of the most iconic stages in the world.

At the beginning of 2019, he joined the electronic music division, otherwise known as Team Disco, in global talent agency CAA's London office. He'd plucked up the courage to introduce himself to the office's co-head, Emma Banks, after spotting her on the Jubilee line en route to a music event one afternoon. She was a widely respected heavyweight of an agent, looking after Florence and The Machine, Katy Perry, Kylie Minogue, the Red Hot Chili Peppers and Muse, to name a few. Shortly after he joined, he signed Italian group Meduza after his friend Sergio, a talent manager, sent him their groundbreaking debut track 'Piece of Your Heart'.

I was teaching yoga full-time in some of the most reputable studios in London, and we were about to buy our first home: a gorgeous two-bedroom flat on the middle floor of a converted Victorian building in Finsbury Park, a neighbourhood twenty minutes north of the city centre. We'd been surfing the crest of a big, beautiful wave since we'd met five years before, and nothing could knock us down. But the deeper our love grew, I realised, the more I stood to lose.

I was blissfully unaware of mortality until the age of eleven. I'd returned home from school on Tuesday 11th September 2001 to see bodies tumbling out of burning buildings on the six o'clock news. Almost three thousand people were killed in the US that day. I couldn't get the images out of my head for weeks.

'Mum!' I'd shout in the middle of the night. She'd come rushing down the corridor and into my bedroom in her nightie. 'Everyone's going to die!'

Fortunately, it was a passing phase. I managed to get through my teens and twenties unscathed, except for the deaths of three grandparents. It was terribly sad, that was a given – but it was sort of how things went at their age. Death, I decided, would be a later problem. I'd be spared decades until I'd need to confront it again.

I tried to convince myself that my fear was just one of the trade-offs of loving somebody so deeply, but I couldn't seem to shake it off. I felt a sense of urgency to take everything in as best as I could while I still had the chance. All the sounds, the music and the colours. His touch, his smell, his taste. I savoured every moment we shared, longing to relive them before they were even over. Every high was tinged with a quiet melancholy, as though I was mourning something I hadn't yet lost. 'It's too good to be true,' I'd often tell my friends. Perhaps it was paranoia, or a hunch, or both. I'd insist that he texted me when he was coming home late at night. I'd refresh the flight tracker page when he was travelling abroad, just in case. I'd save every wristband, every letter, and every card we wrote to each other in a box underneath our bed. And yet despite all the ways I tried to control things, no matter how tightly I grasped, I couldn't help feeling like something bad was about to happen, that he was slipping through my fingers like sand.

5

'It was a hard session tonight,' came Ben's voice from underneath me, muffled by the pillow pressing against his face. 'I'm knackered! I gave those fights my all.'

'Obviously,' I replied. Because that was just Ben. He was never one to do anything half-arsed.

It was a wet February evening in 2019, and he'd just received his blue belt in jiu jitsu at a grading ceremony at his mixed martial arts gym, the London Fight Factory in Shoreditch. He was lying on the bed after practice with a towel wrapped around him, fresh from the shower. Rain drummed loudly against the window as I reached for the jar of coconut oil on the bedside table.

'Have you injured your shoulder?' I asked as I ran my fingers across his left shoulder blade towards his spine. A lump, two centimetres wide, was protruding from his skin.

'Er – I don't think so.'

'Hmm,' I murmured, watching the oil trickle from my fingers and onto his back. 'You've got a lump here. Maybe it's some muscle that hasn't healed properly, or a hernia or something.' I pressed my thumbs into it. 'Can you feel anything?'

'Nope! Nothing.'

I kneaded the lump with my elbow. 'What about now?'

'Still nothing.'

'That's weird. Well, let's just keep an eye on it.' I bent down to kiss the back of his neck then climbed off him. The absence of pain seemed like a good enough reason for us to shrug it off. A month passed, and then another, but when I noticed that the lump hadn't shown any signs of retreating, I suggested he get it checked out.

'It's probably a lipoma,' his local GP assured him. 'A lipoma is a fatty lump and nothing to worry about, but we'll book you in for an ultrasound six weeks from now just to be sure.'

Of course, it couldn't be anything serious. Ben was young, and the picture of health. He exercised five times a week, ate organic food – with the exception of a cheat meal or two at weekends – and drank no more than anybody else.

The evening after the ultrasound in June, I was serving up dinner when I heard the front door click shut.

'You're just in time,' I called out to him as I laid the table. 'How did it go?' I craned my neck to peer down the hallway. 'Ben?'

He forced a smile as he walked towards me.

'I don't really know what to think,' he replied, his lips pursed as he gnawed at the inside of his mouth. He slung his backpack onto the chair under the kitchen counter and pulled his denim jacket off. 'The nurse seemed concerned after she'd looked at it.' She had fast-tracked him for an MRI later that week, and had requested a needle biopsy to remove some of the tissue for testing. 'They only do that if they . . .' He swallowed. 'If they think you've got cancer.'

'Baby,' I replied. I walked over to him and rested my hands on his shoulders. 'They're doctors – they've always got to assume the worst. They're just doing due diligence.' Cancer was one of those unfortunate things that happened to other people – people who were either old or unhealthy. I cupped his face and kissed him on both cheeks. 'Remember what my granny always said? Don't trouble trouble until trouble troubles you.'

As far as grandparents went, I'd have been hard pushed to find a better one than my mum's mum, Iris. She was pint-sized and totally gorgeous, with twinkly blue eyes and a salt and pepper bob, but make no mistake: her petite and delicate frame had no bearing on her strength. Little Granny, as we fondly called her, was just a child when her mum had walked out on her dad, forcing her to grow up fast and mother her three younger siblings. She was the matriarch of my family and I completely adored her. She'd died four months earlier on Valentine's Day.

But not troubling trouble, of course, was a million times easier said than done. Our future had stretched out before us, full of promise. We'd had it all mapped out – a wedding in Ibiza, then a baby – ideally two, but one at the very least. It had felt so certain, so real to me – but now it felt as if it was hanging in the balance, waiting for a verdict that threatened to burn it all to the ground.

At the end of June, we loaded our tent and sleeping bags into the back of our hire car bound for Glastonbury Festival. Ben had booked a couple of artists to play there. The appointment to find out the results of the biopsy was scheduled for the following week, and we welcomed a distraction from our steadily rising anxiety. Anyone who has undergone the diagnostic process for a serious illness will tell you that the wait for the results is a sickening kind of limbo. We were operating entirely on autopilot, present in body but not quite in mind, unable to sync up and keep pace with the world around us. A sense of foreboding hovered over us like a black cloud, the air thick with unspoken fears.

As we watched the headliners perform on the Pyramid Stage, I'd catch Ben staring off into the distance, and wonder what he was thinking about. We'd glance at each other and smile nervously. I tried my hardest to stay positive, but my mind ran away with itself in the quiet moments late at night, away from our friends and the crowds. As we followed the snaking paths that cut through the fields of tents towards our pitch in the early hours of each morning, every step seemed to carry with it the weight of uncertainty and fear. Glastonbury was home to some of our happiest memories. We'd dreamed of sharing it with our children one day. *And we will*, I tried to convince myself. Everything was going to go according to plan.

On Friday 4th July, we travelled to the Royal National Orthopaedic Hospital in Stanmore, north London. The journey took over an hour and a half, with six stops on the Jubilee line from Homerton to Camden Road, a seven-minute walk to Camden Town, nine stops on the Northern line to Edgware station, and the 107 bus towards New Barnet. I counted down the minutes, each one more agonising than the last.

'The doctor is running late,' relayed the receptionist.

'Do you know how late exactly?' I asked.

She glanced at her computer screen and tapped at the keyboard for a moment. 'There's two patients ahead of you.'

I thanked her and sat down next to Ben on one of the blue plastic chairs that lined the corridor. Looking around the reception area, I caught sight of the pamphlets on the rack stuck to the wall opposite. I scanned the text on each in search of the word 'cancer'. There was no mention of it anywhere. I grabbed Ben's hand and let out a slow, forceful exhale, my breath snagging. *That must be a good sign*, I thought. I leafed through a couple of magazines strewn across the coffee table, my eyes glazing over the words. Forty minutes passed, then fifty, when a hairless head sticking out of the top of a crisp white shirt finally appeared round the door.

'Mr Kouijzer?' called out an orotund voice.

We exchanged hellos and stepped inside his office, a vague taste of antiseptic catching in the back of my throat. Fluorescent lights glared off laminated medical charts and accolades, none of which did anything to calm me down.

'Oh,' Ben exclaimed. 'Hi, Andrea.' I turned to find a nurse with wispy white hair perched on the edge of the bed in the corner of the room.

Andrea, I thought. *Where have I heard that name before?* My stomach lurched as I connected the dots – Andrea was the name of the nurse who had taken the biopsy two weeks ago, Ben had told me. What could she possibly be doing here?

'Please,' the doctor said, gesturing for us to sit down. 'My name is Dr Goulding.' I smiled at him as he pulled out his chair and swept up the papers laid out on his desk – a silent plea for some reassurance. His expression was blank, offering no emotional foothold.

'Okay. So, as you know, Ben, we tested the tissue taken from the lump in your back.' He cleared his throat and leaned forwards. 'There's no easy way of saying this, but I'm afraid the results have revealed that you have cancer.'

'Shit,' Ben choked, his voice taut. I turned to look at him, aghast. The colour was draining from his face. Cancer? *No, surely he didn't – he couldn't . . .*

'It's a soft tissue sarcoma,' Dr Goulding continued.

Sarcoma? What the hell was sarcoma?

'It's stage three.'

Fuck. It was definitely cancer. Last night's dinner was rapidly making its way back up my digestive tract. I swallowed. He kept talking but I zoned out. *How? Why?* I thought. *But the biopsy – it was supposed to be a precautionary measure.* 'Just to be on the safe side,' they'd told us. My mind was in overdrive as I sifted through my memories, trying to piece together some evidence – any evidence – that could serve as a rebuttal to his claims.

'Does that sound like a plan?' Dr Goulding asked, his voice distant.

I stared past him, unseeing.

'Yes?' he asked again, louder this time, bringing me to my senses with a jolt. He looked back and forth between the two of us, waiting for an answer. I opened my mouth to reply but nothing came out.

'Mhmm,' Ben uttered feebly. 'Yes. Thank you very much for your time, Dr Goulding. We really appreciate it.' Even in the face of the worst possible news, he still had the capacity to be polite. We stood up in slow motion, nodded our goodbyes, and shuffled out of the room.

'I know it's not the news that either of you were hoping for,' said Andrea's voice from behind us. 'Here,' she said softly, holding a card in her hand. 'Take my contact details. Please don't hesitate to call me if you have any questions – I'll be very happy to help you both.'

'Thank you,' I stammered. I took the card from her and slipped it into my back pocket. We headed towards the exit, bracing ourselves against each other, our legs threatening to buckle under the weight of Dr Goulding's news.

'Let's just stop for a moment, shall we?' I said to him as we stepped outside. We collapsed onto the nearest bench beside the pathway and sat there for a while in stunned silence. I couldn't believe what I'd just heard. I couldn't fathom that life in the hospital grounds seemed to carry on like normal, as if ours hadn't imploded just seconds ago inside. Cancer had come careening into our otherwise beautiful life, scoring a distinct and ugly line right through the middle of it. Now what? Where on earth were we supposed to go from here? I turned to look at Ben, his eyes brimming with tears. *Nature*, I thought. That would do it. Nature would hold the answers – but first, we needed to call our families. We dialled Jean, Christiaan and Nicole, and then my mum and Dougal, each of their voices subdued and shaky as they digested the news. We exchanged some tears and some comforting words and promised to speak again when we got home.

Once we'd summoned the strength to climb to our feet, we left the hospital and took the various buses and trains back towards the city centre. We jumped off at Hampstead station in north London and wandered along the high street in search of something to eat. I paused outside one of the cafes for a moment, gazing through the window at half a dozen pyramids of glossy pastries sitting inside glass domes.

'What would you like to eat?' I asked Ben.

'Er, well. I guess nothing with any sugar in? It's linked to cancer, isn't it?'

'Oh. Yeah. I think you're right . . .' I was sure I'd read somewhere that sugar made cancer cells proliferate. The realisation hit me – we were in a fight against *cancer* now. Things we needn't have thought twice about yesterday suddenly posed a threat. *Fuck!* I was terrified. His guess was as good as mine.

'I just want to eat a sandwich, to be honest, but I probably shouldn't. It's not exactly healthy, is it?'

The other love of Ben's life was a cheese sandwich. 'Friends reunited,' he'd whisper, taking the first bite into a highly anticipated Ploughman's baguette after every jiu jitsu tournament. (For the non-Brits among us, a Ploughman's is a cold meal usually consisting of bread, cheese and fresh or pickled onions. If you're feeling fancy and really want to large it, you might throw some ham, boiled eggs and salad into the mix too.) A cheese sandwich was, without fail, Ben's meal of choice after every night out. Some might even call it a ritual. I had often woken up on a Saturday morning to find breadcrumbs throughout the flat. I'd follow the trail to discover a chopping board and a knife, along with discarded cheese and crisp packets of varying flavours scattered across the kitchen counter. There was never any bread, cheese or crisps in sight. He would polish off the lot and conveniently forget all about it the following morning.

Double fuck.

We ordered a cucumber, celery, kale and ginger juice each before continuing up the road towards the heath. Hampstead Heath spans seven hundred and ninety rambling, hilly acres, with ponds, playgrounds, and ancient woodlands adjoining a seventeenth-century former stately home, Kenwood House, and its estate. Over the years, we'd spent countless sunny afternoons every summer sprawled on a blanket in front of the ponds, eating sandwiches and fresh strawberries we'd picked up at the farmers' market down the road.

We walked past the bathing ponds and turned left, off the path and into the woods towards a nearby oak tree.

'I don't want to die.' He started sobbing suddenly the moment we sat down.

'Oh, Ben,' I cried, throwing my arms around him. 'You won't!' I begged him not to talk like that. We could deal with this, we could *totally* deal with it. This was him, for God's sake. If anyone could beat cancer, it was him. I seized his hands with both of mine. 'What did Dr Goulding say – something about surgery? And radiotherapy? Didn't he mention something about there being no cancer anywhere else? That's positive, isn't it? Something to hold on to, no?'

'Yeah. You're right.' He nodded feebly, wiping away his tears with the back of his hand. 'I've got this.'

6

When we got home we called our families again. We cried some more, comforted each other, then set about devising a plan of action. He would do the surgery and radiotherapy like Dr Goulding had suggested, we decided. The surgery would remove all the cancerous tissue, and the radiotherapy would stop it from coming back. We'd make some small tweaks to his diet, think good thoughts. Then it would all be over and cancer would be a thing of the past. We could move on with our lives. Right? Right. It sounded simple enough – so long as we stuck to the plan and didn't deviate, he'd be fine. *Surely*. A plus B equalled cured. And anyway, Dr Goulding hadn't mentioned a prognosis, so there was no need for us to start catastrophising. This wasn't a life-or-death situation we were dealing with, otherwise he'd have said so. I didn't care to look up any information about the disease online. What would be the point? To do so would plant doubt in my mind, will the worst case into existence. The diagnosis would simply mark a bump in the road, a bad moment in time that we would wipe our hands clean of after treatment.

◆ ◆ ◆

On 22nd July, two weeks later, we returned to the hospital in Stanmore for the surgery, this time with some reinforcement in tow. Jean flew over from Malaga, and Christiaan and Nicole drove down from Nottingham. I hugged them tightly, each of us exchanging nervous smiles. The surgeons, we were told, would attempt to remove the lump and the surrounding muscle and bone tissue, in case any of the cancer cells had spread. It could take a few hours, then he'd need to stay in for a few more days until he was ready to be discharged. We would see him during the hospital's visiting hours and stay at a hotel down the road in the meantime.

Come two o'clock in the afternoon, Ben was ready to be taken down to the anaesthetist's room next door to the operating theatre. I walked alongside the gurney holding his hand as the nurse took him in.

'God,' he said, forcing a smile. 'My heart is pounding.'

'You're going to be okay, my love,' I said, stroking his head. I reminded him that he was in expert hands, that this was a routine procedure for them. I watched, queasy, as the anaesthetist inserted a needle into a vein in his right hand and started to administer the drug. I told him to think of his favourite place, picture us on a beach in Ibiza somewhere.

'Yeahhh,' he murmured, his eyelids getting heavier. 'Sun, saa-and . . .' And with that, it was lights out.

I gave him a kiss and headed back upstairs to the waiting area. Jean, Christiaan, Nicole and I wandered through the grounds together, making the occasional detour back to the hospital canteen for another watery coffee each. Two hours passed, then three. Then four. I kept stealing glances at my watch. Time kept crawling by. It wasn't until five and a half hours later that Andrea finally appeared in the waiting area again. The four of us lunged towards her, our faces etched with worry.

'Good news,' she said with a smile. 'The surgery went well. He's back in his room now and is just coming around from the anaesthetic.'

47

'Thank goodness,' Jean exclaimed as we let out a collective sigh.

In September, once he'd recovered from surgery, he went back to the office, only taking time off work for radiotherapy treatment. We moved into our new flat in Finsbury Park at the end of the month, and, slowly but surely, began to adjust to a new normal. There were no outward signs that he had even *had* cancer in the first place. You'd have only suspected that something serious had happened if you'd noticed the seven-inch scar on his back, or examined the contents of our food cupboards. 'I'll tell everyone it's a shark bite,' he grinned.

Reishi mushroom, Japanese knotweed, medical cannabis and sencha green tea were a few of the dozen or so powders and potions he insisted on taking each morning. 'It's just a precaution,' he'd reassure me, as he measured out each of the powders with fastidious care before popping them into the food blender. I believed him. It was safer that way.

In a bid to make it fun, he invited a different friend to go along to every radiotherapy appointment at the Macmillan Cancer Centre in Camden with him. In mid-November we celebrated the end of treatment at a local pub in Stoke Newington with all of our friends. A CT scan the following month showed no signs of the disease, prompting a cautious optimism in each of us that grew steadily as we edged closer to Christmas. We celebrated with our respective families, and met up the day after Boxing Day at Heathrow airport to catch a plane to Sydney, via Los Angeles. Ben had booked his clients Meduza and Hot Dub Time Machine to play several shows at different festivals throughout Sydney during the first week of January, and our friends Harry and Robyn, who had moved there from London a few years before, had invited us to stay with them. I could barely contain my excitement. The four of us were close friends and had remained in regular contact since the move, but hadn't seen each other for several years.

Ben and I travelled back and then forwards again across time zones, arriving a day and a half later, under-slept and jet-lagged. We trudged towards the taxi rank outside the terminal and took a cab to Bondi, the beachside suburb east of the city centre.

Before long, the car pulled up outside Harry and Robyn's building, a block away from the boardwalk that ran parallel to the beach.

'You're here!' came Harry's familiar voice from behind us as we pulled our suitcases out of the boot of the car. I turned to find him lolloping across the pavement towards us, arms outstretched, grinning from ear to ear. He was dressed in a loose white shirt, taupe linen shorts and sandals. 'It's so good to see you,' he exclaimed.

The three of us hugged and headed inside, suitcases in tow. Robyn was standing at the kitchen counter making a coffee in black Lycra shorts and a matching sports bra, her chestnut brown hair tied back in a bun.

'Oh my God!' she beamed. 'Welcome!' She set down the cafetière and flung her arms around us both. The years apart melted away in the warmth of her familiar hug. No matter the miles between us, our bond would never be diminished. And that, I thought to myself, was the hallmark of true friendship.

We freshened up and headed back outside to wander along the boardwalk, coffees in hand, catching up on all the events that had unfolded between the gaps.

Maybe it was over, I thought to myself as I listened to Ben share how good he felt.

'You look amazing, mate,' Harry insisted, putting his arm around him. The two of them walked ahead and Robyn and I linked arms. Maybe cancer really *was* behind us now. Over ten thousand miles from London, it couldn't have felt any further away as it did in that moment.

A few days later, on New Year's Eve, we ate dinner at a local pizzeria before taking the metro to Milsons Point by Sydney Harbour. A palpable excitement hung in the air as thousands of people poured through the streets. We joined the stream of revellers heading down the hill towards Luna Park, an amusement park right by the water that overlooked Sydney Harbour Bridge. Ben's act, Hot Dub Time Machine, was due to play at the park after midnight.

'Harry?' Ben asked as we set up shop for the fireworks by the water's edge. 'Would you mind taking a photo of us, please? Portrait mode, yeah, mate?' He passed Harry his phone as I laced my arms around him.

'Say cheese!' Harry shouted, his smile waggish.

Tucking strands of flyaway hair behind my ears, I grinned at Harry while Ben fumbled around in his pockets. He broke away from me, and I glanced sideways to find him kneeling by my feet, clutching a small navy box in his hand.

'Lotte Bowser.'

'Yes?' I looked at him, bemused. What was he doing down there? Had he dropped something? He opened the box to reveal something small and sparkly.

'Will you marry me?'

'*What?*' I snorted, cupping my hands over my mouth. I was sure I hadn't heard him properly.

'Will you marry me?' he asked again, his voice more urgent now.

'Oh my God!' I cried. 'Yes!' Of *course* yes. Of course I wanted to spend the rest of my life with him. I'd never felt more sure of anything. He climbed to his feet and our mouths locked in a kiss as Harry and Robyn ran towards us, cheering. 'Oh my God,' I gushed again, as Ben carefully extracted the ring from the box and slid it onto my finger. I held out my hand to study it, wiggling my fingers to catch the sparkle. It was a pavé diamond halo with a round diamond centre set in platinum. 'It's beautiful!'

'Congratulations,' said Robyn, flushed with excitement. The four of us hugged, when suddenly a roar came from all around us.

'Ten, nine, eight,' cried the crowd, their bellows reverberating around the harbour. We spun on our heels to see the countdown projected onto the bridge. 'Five, four, three, two, one!'

Boom. The fireworks erupted, brilliant shades of pink, purple, orange and green swirling in the night sky like cosmic ballet dancers. Tens of thousands of people erupted in spontaneous applause. I looked at Ben, his green eyes all lit up and sparkling, a gorgeous contrast to his sun-kissed skin.

'Let's start as we mean to go on, baby,' he said, kissing me. 'I have a feeling 2020 is going to be the best year yet.'

Every morning for the next week, we woke as the sun rose and headed to Bondi beach to watch the first flock of surfers catch the waves. We travelled north to Byron Bay for a long weekend and explored the local beaches, from Byron to Little Wategos, to the loop around Cape Byron lighthouse nestled between the ocean and hinterland. We watched Meduza and Hot Dub Time Machine play to packed-out crowds in Sydney's city centre. We dined alfresco on fresh barramundi, drank spicy margaritas, and dreamed up ideas for our wedding.

Come mid-January, we returned home with a renewed vigour. Ben went back to the office and I went back to the yoga studios. We spent our weekends creating Pinterest boards with ideas for wedding decorations, taking trips to IKEA to buy kitchenware, and painting our bedroom walls burnt orange. He signed up for the London Marathon in April to raise money for the charity Sarcoma UK, and started running again around Finsbury Park. Cancer was a thing of the past, we decided. The turning of the clock hand come midnight on New Year's Eve had marked a new beginning, wiped the slate clean. 2020 was ours for the taking.

7

On the 26th March, the day after Ben's thirty-sixth birthday, we drove to the hospital in Stanmore again for a routine follow-up scan. Scans were recommended every three to four months for the first two years after treatment. I hadn't given the appointment much thought. In all honesty, in recent months, I hadn't spent much time thinking about cancer at all. So long as I could steer clear of hospitals, I could squash it down, act like none of it had happened in the first place. Ben, on the other hand, was clearly stressed. I knew him well enough to read the signs, even though he tried his best to hide it from me. I attempted to make conversation in the car but he replied with one-word answers. There was a shift in his tone of voice, still gentle but frayed.

'Are you alright?' I asked him as we pulled into the outpatients' car park.

'Yes,' he snapped. 'I just want to get this over with.'

'Ben, it's going to be fine,' I said firmly. His shortness got on my nerves. There was no need for him to start freaking out, not yet. We headed through the entrance and followed the signs to the radiology department. A nurse behind the reception desk pointed to a box of PPE face masks sitting on top of the counter.

'You'll need to wear a mask in compliance with Covid-19 regulations, I'm afraid,' she informed us. 'They're mandatory.'

The coronavirus was steadily making its way through the country, claiming thousands of lives. Just a few days earlier, the prime minister had announced a national lockdown, ordering the nation to close non-essential businesses and stay at home in a bid to reduce the transmission of the virus and protect those among us who were most vulnerable. It was odd – apart from the dwindling supply of toilet roll at our local supermarket, the virus had felt like something of an abstract concept since it had arrived on British soil. I'd downplayed the gravity of it. I didn't think we were at risk. According to the World Health Organisation, it was primarily a concern for older people, or people with pre-existing health conditions. Ben didn't have a pre-existing condition. He was cancer free – the last scan had proved it. We would do our bit to protect others, of course, just like everyone else – and willingly at that. Besides, the prospect of staying at home with Ben until further notice was hardly bleak. We'd longed for days off work, just the two of us. We disinfected our hands, took a mask each and sat down in the waiting area. After a while, another nurse appeared and called Ben's name. He disappeared around the corner with her, returning ten minutes later.

'All done,' he mumbled behind his mask.

I looked at the clock hanging on the wall behind reception, each tick amplifying the drumroll of anxiety in my chest. Fifteen minutes passed, when a doctor I hadn't seen before entered the waiting area.

'Ben?' he asked. 'We'd like to do a CT scan. The results of the X-ray came back indeterminate.'

We glanced sideways at each other. Indeterminate? What the hell did that mean?

'Okay.' Ben nodded, his voice trembling. The doctor led us through several snaking corridors to another corner of the hospital. I sat down outside the imaging room as Ben followed the doctor inside. A handful of patients were waiting to be seen, each of them exchanging whispered conversations and worried glances with their loved ones.

He reappeared some time later with instructions on how to get to the sarcoma unit, where Dr Goulding would see us to discuss the results.

'He's late. *Again*,' I hissed, as we sat in the same waiting area as the summer before.

Thirty minutes passed, then forty.

'What's the hold-up?'

Ben looked at me and shook his head, by now unable to speak.

I stood and paced up and down the corridor. Gurneys rolled past, their wheels whining against the polished linoleum. The sound made the hairs on the back of my neck stand on end. It was impossible not to think about cancer here, to not let my imagination run away with itself.

Stay calm, I willed myself.

Suddenly, Dr Goulding's door opened.

'Ben?' he called out.

'Hi,' we uttered. We walked into his room and sat down.

'How are you doing today?' he asked.

We nodded at him.

'How the bloody hell do you think we're doing?' I wanted to reply. He'd picked the worst possible time for small talk. I just wanted him to put an end to our torment.

'Okay,' he said flatly. 'I believe my colleague informed you that the X-ray was inconclusive. It's not good news, I'm afraid. The cancer has spread to both of your lungs.'

'FUCK,' we exclaimed in unison.

No! I seized Ben's hand as white-hot adrenaline coursed through my veins.

'It's terminal.'

There it was: a pronouncement of a single word that flipped my organs inside out, delivered with a cold, stark precision. There was no softening the impact, no attempt to cushion the fall.

No, no, no, I screamed inside. My legs started shaking, the floor threatening to give way under me. I wanted to escape, to unzip myself from my skin somehow and crawl out of it.

'Some patients can live for years,' he went on.

I searched the room, desperate. The window above the filing cabinet was open. Could I squeeze myself out unnoticed? Into a black hole, never to resurface?

'But I'll be frank with you,' came his voice again from somewhere. 'The reality is that at some point, this will kill you.'

He kept talking but I couldn't hear him, couldn't make out the words. A stream of indeterminate syllables kept tumbling from his mouth, all blurred together. *Terminal*, he'd said. The disease was terminal. The word rang violently in my head like a thunderclap, my blood pounding in my ears. Lung metastases, he'd said – several of them – all the while an insidious virus that affected the host's respiratory tract lingered in the air, lingered on the *surfaces* for all we knew. *Fuck, fuck, FUCK!*

Just like that, a hole had opened up beneath my feet, and my life as I had come to know and love it fell right through.

We drove home in a stupor, neither of us saying much. What could even be said? For the first time in my life, I couldn't seem to find any words. They'd always come so easily to me, so naturally, but now I was mute. Lost. 'It's going to be okay, Ben,' was about all I could manage, resting my hand on his leg in a pathetic attempt to comfort him. Would it be, though? My voice was weak and unconvincing. I'm not sure I even believed it myself.

We fell through our front door and onto the sofa some time later, each taking it in turns to cry, before picking up our phones to break the news to our families. They couldn't hide their devastation,

my mum weeping quietly, Dougal's voice breaking in the background. Ben's mum, Jean, was at home alone in Malaga, tending
to the flowerbeds on her terrace when we called. My heart shattered
all over again, but this time for her. What must it have felt like to
be told that your child had been given a death sentence? And to be
thousands of miles away, unable to do anything at all? I wanted to
reach through the phone and hold her.

'We'll get through this,' Christiaan offered, his voice soft yet
resolute. We couldn't forget that Ben had options: the surgery, the
chemo, all of the other treatments we'd yet to discover. We wiped
our eyes and hung up, drifting listlessly through the next few hours
until the evening came.

I'd hoped that the darkness would offer us some respite, but it
only made it ten times worse. As night fell, I lay in bed staring at the
ceiling, the weight of terror pressing down on me. My thoughts spun
in a web of chaos. I tried to fall asleep but my mind kept racing. All
I kept thinking was, how would I go on living in the absence of the
person I knew I couldn't live without? I simply wouldn't. I couldn't.
What would even be the point in being alive anymore anyway? It was
me and him, Team Botty. I no longer knew the version of me that
had existed before him. She was a stranger to me now. There were so
many things to do still, places to see. We had plans.

I rolled over to find him fast asleep next to me. I lifted up his
t-shirt and gently ran my hand over his ribcage, feeling the rise and
fall of his breath, steady and calm. I wanted to carve the cancer out
of him somehow and make it all go away. What must it have felt
like to be in his shoes? To want to live so badly, but to exist inside
a body that wouldn't play ball? We needed a miracle. If there was a
god, now felt as good a time as any to start praying. I pulled back
the duvet, slipped out of bed and tiptoed into the living room. I
dropped to my knees and crawled across the carpet towards the
small wooden chest in the corner.

'Please,' I begged, kneeling in front of the chest, my hands clasped together in prayer. 'If you're real, please don't take the person I love most away from me. I'll do anything.' I chewed at the sleeves of my dressing gown, attempting to buffer the sound of the sobs spewing from my mouth, so laboured and awkward that, before long, I completely exhausted myself. I lay there motionless for a while, listening, hoping for an answer or a revelation to appear out of the darkness from somewhere. There was nothing except for the quiet gurgling of the fridge in the next room. 'Why did this happen to us?' I asked no one. Ben was a good person. Bad things weren't supposed to happen to good people.

I realised that I couldn't just lie on the carpet all night, prostrated. Hopelessness would drown me. I needed to hold on to something, *anything* to keep my head above water – not just for my sake, but for Ben's. I pushed myself up to my feet, fumbled for the light switch and glanced over to the bookcase by the sofa. On one of the shelves stood a pile of books about spirituality and self-development that I'd bought years ago while doing my yoga teacher training. I guess you could say that yoga was my gateway into spirituality. All of the yamas and niyamas had sparked my curiosity, and, eager to learn more, I bought the books that had appeared at the top of my Google search – Paulo Coelho's *The Alchemist*, Michael Singer's *The Untethered Soul*. I walked over to the bookcase, pulled Louise Hay's *The Power Is Within You* down, and started flicking through its pages. One of the resounding sentiments that I'd continued to come across over the years was that our thoughts shaped our reality – that everything in our external environment was a manifestation of our internal environment. That if we wanted good things to happen, we had to think good things – and then, *poof!* As if by magic, they would happen. The universe would provide. 'Maybe,' I wondered, tracing my fingers along the ink, 'maybe all of that led me *here.*' Maybe all of *this* was happening for a reason, for a greater purpose that would only be revealed to us in time.

I pulled my laptop out from underneath the sofa and sat down at the dining table. Blinking away the sleep from my eyes, I typed 'terminal illness survivor stories' into Google and pressed 'Enter'. I clicked through the pages to discover hundreds of stories.

In 2002, lymphoma had metastasized throughout Anita Moorjani's body. Her organs shut down and she entered into a coma. Thirty hours later, she woke up. The tumours had shrunk by seventy per cent within just four days, and within five weeks, she was cancer free. *Cancer. Free.*

I clicked on another – a man called Eben Alexander was placed into a coma in 2008, after suffering what should have been a fatal case of bacterial meningitis. His doctors gave him a two per cent chance of survival. A week later he emerged from the coma, and made a full recovery within a few months.

'Oh my God,' I mouthed, astonished. 'This could be Ben.'

I descended down a rabbit hole of research for the next couple of hours, digging up countless books, podcasts and documentaries, all of which spoke of the link between the power of the mind and healing. This was it. A way out – I'd found it! The internet had opened up new vistas of possibility. Staring back at me was cold, hard evidence – irrefutable evidence, in fact – that even in the face of the bleakest prognosis lay the possibility of a different outcome. I felt an ember of hope inside of me. It was a cautious hope – the flame flickering amidst my uncertainty – but still, it was tangible. And that was something.

Russian novelist Fyodor Dostoevsky once wrote that 'to live without hope is to cease to live'. Hope gives us something to stay alive for. It fuels the belief that better days can and will come, even when the circumstances don't look good at all.

I shut the lid of my laptop and sank back into my chair, exhausted but emboldened by my findings. Ignoring the prognosis altogether was the only way forward. Better yet – *defying* the prognosis, just like Anita and Eben had, was the only way forward. The doctors were wrong. He could survive this. I would not lie down and simply wait for him to die. I would learn everything there was to learn about cancer, and I would not stop until he was healed.

8

Our families and closest friends all agreed that a world without Ben was not an option. The thought of it was too unbearable to even entertain, so we wouldn't – or at least, they wouldn't in front of me. In the days that followed the diagnosis, I threw myself head first into the role of his caregiver with a kind of dogged determination, doing anything and everything I possibly could to learn more about cancer and support him. I set about fashioning a makeshift altar on top of the chest in our living room. A bronze statue of Ganesha that Ben had bought in Hampi, India was the centrepiece, surrounded by candles and crystal quartz. I decorated every door and mirror in our flat with fluorescent Post-it notes. I wrote a mantra on each one in bold black letters that read, 'I trust in my journey, I am grateful for my healing. I am healthy, I am healed, I am whole.' If our ideas, thoughts, words and actions could influence the course of events in the material world, then we had to believe they could change the outcome of his disease.

Captions appeared on my Instagram feed several times a day – 'Life is happening for you, not to you' – the words laid on top of a handstand showcasing the latest Lululemon leggings and the arse that filled them. 'Where attention goes, energy flows,' said another over smashed avocado on toast. The words seemed to reach me at a time I needed them the most. The universe was listening.

I researched the optimal diet for a stage four cancer patient. I borrowed Chloe's juicer and turned the kitchen counter into a production line of vegetable juices: beetroot, carrot, ginger and lemon, and cucumber, celery and spinach, on rotation. Annie and Will took it in turns with my friend Victoria to deliver fresh batches to us on the days I couldn't summon the energy to make any. Ben's colleagues from CAA, Jen and Ben, ran errands for us. One of my best friends, Gee, dropped food shopping round. I connected with other cancer survivors online, each of whom were thriving on cocktails of alternative medicine shown to have anti-cancer properties. I copied their protocol meticulously, ordering lists upon lists of herbal supplements and off-label drugs from suspect overseas suppliers online, like statins and dewormers for cats and dogs. Every morning, I checked the lists stuck to the back of the kitchen cupboard door, and set about pulling all the bottles and packets of pills and powders I had ordered down onto the kitchen counter. I separated the doses for both morning and evening, and made a mental note of which ones needed to be taken on an empty stomach. I made herbal teas and potions. I ordered half a dozen books about healing from disease. I Covid-proofed the flat, disinfecting every last thing to cross the threshold of our front door; stacks of cloths, masks and rubber gloves piled high. We pulled tarot cards together, I reached out to shamans and energy healers. I made us meditate for hours on end, writing diary entries from our future selves on our wedding day. I imagined which parts of him I would see in the face of our firstborn – maybe the dimple in his chin, or the little gap between his two front teeth.

I tried to convince myself that it was really that simple. But it wasn't. We were ordinary people catapulted into an uncharted medical landscape, and the maelstrom of information was dizzying. Research on malignant peripheral nerve sheath tumours was horrifyingly scarce, we learned. According to their website, less than two per cent of Cancer Research UK's annual budget went towards sarcoma research. Apparently, sarcomas accounted for less than one per cent of all adult solid malignant cancers, and peripheral nerve sheath tumours just five to ten per cent of that one per cent. Great. As luck would have it, we were dealing with an incredibly rare and difficult one. The only known options were few and far between: surgery, chemotherapy, and if he was eligible, then immunotherapy – but even then, none of these things would actually cure his disease. The best outcome we could hope for was more time, but still, Ben stood far less of a chance of actually achieving that outcome than most. We were thrust from one doctor to the next – oncologists, haematologists and pulmonologists – each of whom only looked at one piece of the puzzle, none of whom seemed to swap any notes. I tried to make my own during every call and consultation, furiously scribbling down words – pulsus paradoxus, p53 activity, MCH1 and CDK4/6 inhibitors – but none of them made any sense. With the help of friends far and wide, we gathered a second team of private doctors in the UK, US and Germany in the hope that, together, they could find the silver bullet that would cure his disease – but it only made our confusion worse. I tried my best to advocate for him, to decode all the scientific papers and medical jargon they sent my way, but while I'd always been passionate about learning, I was a French Studies graduate, for Christ's sake – cancer science was well beyond my remit.

'I think I need to do it,' Ben said, his eyes narrowing in deep thought.

It was April, and we'd just hung up the phone to Dr Newman, the sarcoma specialist at the University College of London hospital in Camden. She'd assured us that surgery was a common treatment for lung metastases. It could improve his chances of surviving, but – and there was always a but, I'd come to learn – it might impact his ability to bounce back after other treatments down the line too, like chemotherapy.

'We've got to try everything we can, don't you think?'

I agreed, knowing full well that we couldn't afford to mess it up, but there was no way of knowing whether it would work or not until after he'd tried it. Every decision was a roll of the dice of the worst possible kind. If he was one of the lucky ones, it *might* improve his chances of surviving like Dr Newman had said. Or, it might make the disease accelerate faster, according to Dr Google. Don't do the surgery, and the disease will definitely spread and he will die anyway. Damned if you do and damned if you don't.

The surgery was scheduled for the start of May at the Royal Brompton hospital in Chelsea, south-west London, five weeks after Dr Goulding had shared the news that the cancer had metastasised. Dr Newman assured us Ben would be in good hands: the Royal Brompton was a specialist heart and lung hospital with some of the best doctors in the country.

A few days before the surgery, Ben started complaining about breathing difficulties. The medical team at the hospital suggested he go in early so they could run some tests. I waved him goodbye from our doorstep as he climbed into the back of Annie and Will's car. The two of them had been quarantining together and had offered to drive Ben to the hospital so I could rest. I watched the car inch towards the crossroads in the morning traffic and eventually turn the corner, before heading back inside and bursting into tears. I felt terrified and desperately alone. The team had told us that he would need to stay in hospital to recover from the surgery for a week at the very least. Now, we were facing a minimum of a week and a half apart. I needed him, and he needed me, but the lockdown restrictions were still in place and there were no exceptions for people facing serious illnesses – not even for terminal ones.

A CT scan showed that he'd developed a pleural effusion – a build-up of excess fluid between the layers of tissue that line the lungs and chest cavity. There was so much fluid in his chest that his left lung had completely collapsed. It had pushed his heart out of place, and had caused his right lung to operate at half its usual capacity. A drain was inserted into his chest to remove the fluid. He stayed in intensive care for the first three days, before moving to a private room on the fifth floor. A couple of days later, he was considered fit enough for surgery.

'I've just been scrolling through our photos,' he texted me an hour before he was due to be taken down to the operating theatre. 'I'm so grateful for all the amazing memories we've made together – and all the amazing memories we are yet to make!'

'Ugh, I can't WAIT to marry you, babe,' I replied. 'I can't wait to make our babies!'

'Me neither.' A photo came through of him propped up in his hospital bed. His hair was tied up in a bun, wild tufts of brown frizz breaking out from under his headphones. His eyes were bloodshot, his cheeks soaked with tears. 'I'm feeling so emotional.'

'I understand, Benny. I am too. I'll be right there with you, okay? When you're having the anaesthetic, I want you to go to your happy place again. Imagine we're sprawled on some sun loungers in front of the ocean, amazing music playing in the background. Imagine I'm there, holding your hand.' I told him I loved him, that he wasn't alone, that I'd speak to him on the other side – but my words felt woefully inadequate. I ought to have been able to set up camp next to his hospital bed. I wanted to take his mind off things, to comfort him when he felt scared.

For the next eight hours, I tried to keep my anxiety at bay by busying myself with things to do around the flat. I pulled all the furniture away from the walls, hoovered and wiped the skirting boards. I rearranged the contents of the kitchen cupboards twice over, cleaned inside the fridge. I pulled my clothes out from my chest of drawers and folded them again. I ran a hot bath and made myself an elaborate dinner, and FaceTimed Mum and Dougal. By nine o'clock in the evening, I was whipped up into a frenzy when, finally, the hospital called. It was the surgeon. The tumours were so deep that he had only managed to remove part of the cancer.

'Oh,' I mumbled. It wasn't exactly the news I'd been hoping for.

'It's okay, my love,' I reassured Ben over FaceTime the next morning. 'Please feel encouraged. *Some* of the cancer is still something – it's still a step in the right direction.' I told him I loved him, and asked him to send me his gratitude list for the day, before hanging up the phone.

Today I'm grateful for:

Being alive after surgery.

The overwhelming support from my family and friends.

Knowing we've made incredible progress towards me being disease free.

Knowing every day now is one day closer to going home.

He stayed in hospital for the next week recovering from surgery. Every other day, I filled up a tote bag with homemade juices, food and snacks I'd picked up from our local organic grocery shop – bone broths, toasted nori, nuts, dark chocolate, avocados, apples and carrots, and his favourite sourdough tuna sandwiches – before catching the Tube to High Street Kensington station.

'Be careful, baby,' he texted me as I made my way through the Underground. He'd felt the need to caution me before I left the house every time, and I understood why. The journey was fifteen stops on the Piccadilly line to Earl's Court, and then the District line straight through. Every moment I spent outside the safety of our four walls, the greater the chances were of coming into contact with the coronavirus. But he didn't need to worry, I assured him, because London had turned into a ghost town. The trains were empty except for the odd key worker and masked traveller I made sure to steer clear of. The streets, once packed with commuters, shoppers and tourists, were eerily quiet. I handed the bag over to the security guard manning the entrance with detailed instructions of how to locate Ben inside, then watched him descend into the bowels of the hospital, bag in hand. I stood on the corner of Sydney Street below Ben's ward, waiting for him to appear at his window on the fifth floor. I watched as he motioned 'cheers' with a sandwich or flask of broth in his hand, and waved at me from behind the glass.

Until his surgery, we'd kept the news about the terminal diagnosis private, only telling our families and immediate circle of friends. But now, we needed help. We wanted to explore other options outside of the NHS that we'd come across online, like genetic testing and targeted immunotherapy treatments, but they could easily exceed tens of thousands of pounds. Together with his family, we wrote a message on the fundraising platform GoFundMe, sharing the news of the metastases and our hopes to find a cure:

> *There are other forms of treatment, targeted therapies and immunotherapies, that can in some cases have better outcomes that we want to explore after surgery. Eligibility for these depends on certain genetic mutations which need to*

be tested for using expensive molecular testing and DNA sequencing, something that is not available as standard through the NHS. If I have certain genetic mutations, I might be eligible for some of these more promising treatments, and maybe even beat this thing!

Whilst I'm not turning my back on the NHS, who have been amazing in so many ways up until this point, we need to form the right team of people, do the necessary testing and create an individualised treatment plan for me, no matter what or where in the world this takes place.

I just don't have the financial resources to do all of this alone.

I realise this is probably the worst time ever to be fundraising. Not just because the financial implications of Covid-19 are hitting everybody hard, but also because there are so many other important causes out there that need your help.

Why donate to me rather than the NHS, or one of the many Covid relief efforts? Why do I deserve money from anybody when there are hundreds of thousands of people suffering around the world? What makes me so special? Honestly, these are all questions I've been going over again and again in my mind.

But I have to ask. If I don't ask, you won't know that I need help.

Following the encouragement of close friends and family, I have created this Gofundme page where you can give as much or as little as you feel able.

Your donations will help me to fund the molecular testing and consultations with specialists who are using forward-thinking treatments to help people like me have better outcomes. The molecular testing is likely to cost £20,000 and I will also need to take an extensive list of supplements and medications. We are grateful to have found, and to be communicating with, someone with a very similar diagnosis to me who is successfully shrinking her tumours using a non-toxic supplement and medication protocol that would cost around £1,500 pcm.

So for my molecular testing, the guidance of these specialists and for a year's worth of the current supplement & medication protocol, I'm looking to raise £50,000. If targeted treatments do become an option as well, this can cost a lot more, and at the moment I'm unsure as to how much.

I appreciate these are big numbers and this is going to be a big challenge, but the advice we've had from people who've been in a similar position to me is 'whatever you do, don't let money be a barrier to getting the right treatment'.

I appreciate that not everybody is in a position to donate money, but there may be other ways you can help me, even just by sharing my story, in case somebody that you know is in a position to help.

These have been the most challenging weeks of my life and I am so grateful for all of the support I've had from friends, family and colleagues so far. I cry every day due to the acts of kindness.

Thanks for taking time to read my story.

Ben x

9

The moment the fundraising page went live the day after the surgery, I collapsed onto the sofa, relieved. Sharing the news meant that we could finally set down some of the burden we'd been carrying around in secret. I lay on the sofa, dragging my thumbs across the screen of my phone every few minutes to refresh the link. Another hundred pounds was donated, then another thousand. The number went up and up and up, and within a matter of hours, we'd exceeded the target. Hundreds of people shared the link and donated – from family and friends, to CAA colleagues and artists and industry associates. To acquaintances we met once on a dance floor, or during our travels in far-flung corners of the world, to friends of friends and friends of *theirs* – total strangers we'd never even met before. The response far outstripped our expectations. I was floored. I called Ben, who was sitting alone in his hospital room in floods of tears.

'It's a testament to you, my love,' I told him, wiping my eyes with the back of my hand. He'd spread so much love and joy throughout his life. He'd given so much to so many people, and now it was his turn to receive something back. That day, it felt as if the whole world was carrying us, lifting us up.

◆ ◆ ◆

A month later, Ben was due to attend a follow-up appointment at the Macmillan centre to discuss the latest scan results post-surgery. An exception to the Covid-19 regulations was made for caregivers accompanying terminally ill patients who were about to receive their scan results. After passing the Covid screening at the entrance, we headed upstairs towards the outpatients' department.

Before long, a voice came from around the corner of the waiting area, calling Ben's name. I recognised the voice – I'd heard it on the phone half a dozen times over the last few weeks. We stood up and followed it, to find a short, middle-aged woman with dark brown hair standing in the doorway next to a sign that read 'Dr Newman'.

She wasn't quite what I'd expected – or, perhaps more truthfully, what I'd hoped for. I searched her face for a sign to hold on to. A glimmer of positivity maybe, but there was nothing. The corners of her mouth barely lifted at all.

The cancer was still growing, she told us – and rapidly. I clung to the edges of my seat, terrified. What did that mean exactly? The next step would be to start three rounds of the chemotherapy drug doxorubicin as soon as possible, but it may or may not work. 'I'll be brutally honest with you. The type of cancer you have is known to be chemo-resistant. We won't know whether the treatment has worked or not until we do a scan after the third round in nine weeks' time.'

She kept talking as if Ben wouldn't survive. Her tone was flat, nonchalant, as though she didn't care much either way. Anger fermented in my blood. How could she be so apathetic? Didn't she realise all we stood to lose? *Fuck you*, I uttered silently as we said our goodbyes.

The first cycle of chemo was scheduled for mid-June, once he'd recovered properly from the lung surgery. In the meantime, we decided to use the funds raised to test the tissue of the tumour removed last summer, in the hope that the results would reveal a genetic mutation and confirm his eligibility for a targeted immunotherapy drug.

The chemo drug doxorubicin was nicknamed the 'red devil', and for good reason. It was bright red in colour like Kool-Aid, and ran the gamut of every possible side effect you could think of, including hair loss, fevers, chills, vomiting, mouth sores, shortness of breath, joint pain, stomach pain, infertility and irreversible heart damage that, in some cases, could lead to heart failure and kill you.

'Let's shave it all off,' Ben said to me in the bathroom one morning, his hair falling to his shoulders in gorgeous, chaotic ringlets. We needed to grasp on to something positive, to take back a sense of control.

'Let's do it, baby,' I replied as I ran my hands through it. 'It's just hair – it'll grow back before you know it, and anyway, you don't need it. Let's be honest – with a face this beautiful, you can pull anything off.'

He sat on a dining chair on top of a bin bag in the living room with a towel over his shoulders as I separated his hair into eight sections. I tied the sections into ponytails and plaited them, before carefully cutting them off with a pair of scissors I pulled from the kitchen drawer. I ran his electric razor over his head, his eyes welling with tears as he read out loud information about a charity he'd found online that provided wigs to children suffering with cancer.

'It's worth losing it all, knowing a little girl can use it to have hair again.'

My heart welled. I couldn't have loved him more than I did in that moment, his desire to help others more important than any pain or fear he felt.

◆ ◆ ◆

On the morning of his first chemo appointment in the third week of June, we took the Victoria line to Warren Street station and headed towards the Macmillan centre.

'Stay strong, my love,' I offered as we approached the entrance, pulling my mask down to kiss him. 'It's going to be okay. Remember, this is a routine procedure for them. There's nothing to fear, alright? I'll come back in a couple of hours to pick you up.'

He gave me a thumbs up, and although everything besides his eyes was hidden behind his face mask, I knew him well enough to know that they told a different story: he was petrified.

I watched as he wandered through the revolving doors, gentle and composed. He walked up the stairs, one hand holding the rail, the hem of his favourite festival kimono that he'd bought in Ibiza billowing behind him. He'd wanted to dress up, to remind himself of happier times, a feeble attempt to infuse some lightheartedness into an otherwise horrifying situation. A sob snagged in my throat as he disappeared at the top of the stairs. It was a desperately sad sight. I turned left on University Street and headed towards the Cotton Rooms hotel nearby to drop off our bags. The hotel was reserved for cancer patients undergoing certain chemo treatments, in case they needed urgent medical attention overnight.

'I'm so excited to make a little us,' he texted me a little while later. I was standing in the queue for the checkout at Wholefoods supermarket, holding a basket full of food and snacks for dinner. 'I've been imagining the moment we hold her for the first time. We're both just staring at her in awe, crying tears of joy.'

'I can't wait, baby,' I replied. I already knew what she would look like. Her hair would be a blend of his curls and my colour. Her eyes were hazel, somewhere in-between ours, and her skin olive, just like his.

A couple of hours later, I picked him up outside the entrance where I'd left him.

'Hi, Benny,' I smiled, attempting to hide the shock on my face as he stumbled towards me in a daze.

'Hey,' he drawled, his voice slurred as if he'd been knocking back pints all afternoon. 'Oh, this is for you.' He reached into his trouser pocket and pulled out a small laminated card. On it were the colours red, orange and green. 'If you have any of the red side effects,' it read, 'you must contact your advice line immediately. They may ask you to go to the hospital or call 999.' I scanned the list. Chest pain, difficulty breathing, generally unwell, shivery episodes or flu-like symptoms, temperature above 37.5 degrees, below 36 degrees. Vomiting, diarrhoea, bleeding. Swollen or painful legs, sore mouth that stops you eating or drinking. I was scared shitless. His life was on the line, and I felt single-handedly responsible for it.

I put my arm around him as we slowly made our way towards the hotel. I sat him down on the bed, pulled off his trainers, and helped him get undressed and into his pyjamas. I lay wide awake while he slept, my eyes glued to the number on the digital thermometer sticking out from under his armpit.

The following morning at eleven o'clock, we checked out of the hotel and took a taxi back home, where Ben would spend the next three weeks recovering until he was due in again for the second round of chemo.

By mid-July, the results from the molecular testing came back: the tumour samples showed no signs of a mutation that made him eligible for immunotherapy. The chemo, then, was our only hope. Another devastating blow. The side effects of doxorubicin soon took hold of him: chills, sweats, nausea, vomiting and pain – unbearable pain.

'I've never felt anything like it,' he moaned, lying curled in a ball on the sofa one morning. 'My head is on fire. My muscles, bones – everything is hurting.'

Time seemed to warp in-between each round of treatment. Lockdown restrictions had started to ease, with pubs and restaurants and non-essential shops reopening. I craved the feeling of normality, longed to do ordinary things that ordinary thirty-year-olds did, like spending time with friends, going shopping, eating dinner out. Except I couldn't. Ben was terrified to set foot outside in case he caught the virus, and rightly so. The chemo, we were told, would decimate his already compromised immune system. The most vulnerable among us were instructed to stay indoors.

Instead, our families took it in turns to visit – Mum and Dougal, Christiaan and Nicole, and Jean. They'd quarantine for two weeks before their visit, and sit at the far end of our living room in rubber gloves and masks, giving us both as wide a berth as possible, just in case. I was desperate to be held, to collapse into my mum's arms and cry, let everything I'd been holding in, out. But at least it was something, I thought. I cherished it: being in the same room together. In the face of death, the little things, I'd come to realise, no longer felt all that little.

The days rolled into nights and the nights rolled into days. When the sun was up, I could busy myself with things to do – cooking, cleaning, tidying, nursing. I could remain in denial, cling on to my sense of control. I tried to puncture the monotony of lockdown, to salvage whatever semblance of normal was left. I taught my morning yoga classes on Zoom. We played cards together, listened to music, and watched our favourite films. We had video calls with our family and friends. We meditated and wrote bucket lists – return to Ibiza, get married, have children. I tried to keep our spirits high. But by the time the night came, I was paralysed by fear again. I'd stare at the ceiling for what felt like hours on end, until I eventually succumbed to a fitful sleep. Nightmares would jolt me awake, and I'd search for him on the other side of the bed. My fingers would trace the scar that curled under his left arm like a horseshoe. I'd rest my hand on his ribcage for a while to make sure he was still breathing. I'd wonder what it would feel like to lie there in an empty bed, to reach across to a hollow space where the contours of his body ought to be. I wanted to wake him up, to have him comfort me, only I couldn't. He didn't need to carry that burden and to feel my fear too, as well as his own. I wanted to ring my mum, my sister – anyone – but since we were stuck inside our flat, there was nowhere I could go to talk out of earshot. There was no one for me to turn to.

With every round of chemo, the onslaught of side effects grew more merciless. A relentless agony took root in my soul as I looked on, a helpless bystander, longing to bear some of his pain. I rushed him to A&E half a dozen times with a suspected neutropenic fever. Neutrophils are a type of white blood cell that act as the immune system's first line of defence. For cancer patients like Ben, a low neutrophil count or neutropenia was considered life threatening. He spent a total of thirty days in hospital, left to his own devices to stare at the four walls of his room.

I tried to ignore the indisputable truth that he was growing weaker with every hospital admission, tried to ignore the skin stretched across his bones, sagging in parts. I did everything that I could possibly think of to care for him. I bathed him in Epsom salt, I rubbed aromatherapy oils into his feet. I dressed him and undressed him and dressed him again. I organised his daily protocol of medicines and pored over recipe books, cooking him whatever he wanted to eat. I fed him, stroked him, whispered words of affirmation in his ear. I tried to get inside his head, to feel what he was feeling.

I did it willingly, and I'd have done it for another fifty years if given the chance. But as the days wore on, my spirit grew weaker. Ever since Dr Goulding had delivered the news that the disease had metastasised, life had felt like one unrelenting, white-knuckle roller coaster ride with no emergency stop button. Every waking moment of every day was spent either thinking about or talking about cancer. I'd become stultified by following the same tedious routine day in, day out. I'd been brought to my knees time and time again, forced to endure blow after blow after blow. I felt so desperate, so demoralised, so utterly fucking sick of it all, that I'd sometimes catch myself daydreaming about another life – a life that felt normal, where I wasn't a caregiver to somebody who was terminally ill. I wanted to jump off the ride and run – far, far away. Away from Covid, from his disease, from the grief that had begun to eat at me as I watched him waste away in front of my very own eyes. I hated myself for it.

10

'What if I'm not here a few months from now, Lotte?' he cried one evening. He was slumped in the beanbag in the living room, his body swallowed up by a mound of pine green velvet. The words hit me like a sucker punch to the gut, knocking the air right out of my lungs. It was the first time I'd ever heard him entertain the idea of actually dying out loud.

'No, Ben,' I pleaded, throwing myself onto the floor next to him. My voice was shrill and panic-stricken. 'You can't think like that,' I cried. I kissed his hands and searched his eyes. 'You will be, my love! I promise. You've got to stay strong, to focus on your healing, remember?' I wiped his tears with my sleeve and kissed him again. I buried my head into his chest and felt his hand flop onto my back, his touch weak. Defeated. I felt my eyes becoming hot, tears threatening to boil over. *Not now, Lotte*, I thought, blinking furiously. I looked up. 'What can I do for you, baby? How can I make you feel better? Would you like me to run you a bath?'

'Yes, please,' he nodded, his voice small.

I climbed to my feet and went into the bathroom. I searched for the bucket of Epsom salt under the bathtub and turned on the taps. What if he didn't want to be strong, or brave, or any of the other things everyone had told him to be? I thought to myself as I pulled the lid off and dragged the small plastic cup through the salt. What if what he really needed was permission to feel scared? Permission to accept his prognosis, to stop fighting? I had never thought to consider it until that moment. The only narrative I'd ever heard when it came to cancer was that you had to fight it. A cancer patient had to be strong and brave and positive. I tipped the salt in and sat on the edge of the bath for a while, head in hands and staring at the floor. It wasn't like I could give him the space to be anything but those things even if I wanted to, because I couldn't bear to spend even a second entertaining the thought of him not being around. If he died, I thought, his death would surely be the death of me.

I wandered back into the living room and helped him to his feet.

'Let's get you undressed.'

He closed the lid of the toilet and sat down as I helped him out of his clothes. By now, it was a struggle to even lift up his arms. He stood and leaned against me as he climbed into the tub, the sight of him naked making me feel things I couldn't act on anymore. It had been so long since we had enjoyed each other in that way, I thought to myself as I knelt down beside him. I dragged the plastic cup through the water and poured it over his head.

'Mmm,' he muttered with a half smile. 'This is one of the upsides of having no hair.'

'Oh, baby,' I replied softly. *There he goes again . . . Always searching for the positives*, I thought. I lathered the sponge sitting on the side of the bath with a bar of lavender soap and pressed it gently against his skin, careful not to hurt him. 'I don't understand this,' I uttered quietly. 'I just don't understand. Why did *you* have to get cancer, Ben? Of all people. *You* . . .'

He looked at me and shrugged. 'Why *not* me?'

◆ ◆ ◆

On 18th August, we took a taxi to the Macmillan centre for a follow-up appointment with Dr Newman. You'd have thought that once you'd been for a certain amount of scans and appointments you'd get used to the ice-cold dread that coils itself around your chest like a boa constrictor. You don't – or at least, I didn't. I walked into her office stiff with fear.

'Unfortunately the chemo hasn't worked,' she said, peering at us through thick-rimmed glasses balancing on top of her face mask. 'I'm really sorry, but at this point, there's nothing else we can do for you. If there's anything you want to do, I suggest you go do it now.'

A cold numbness washed over me. I was there but not really, watching myself above myself, like a surveillance camera suspended in the corner of the room.

'Go and take a holiday. And then . . .'

I wanted to ram my fingers into my ears and drown out her voice. *LA LA LA! Shut the fuck UP!*

'Have a think about getting your affairs in order, and making arrangements.' She slid a leaflet across the desk and I glanced down at it. 'End of Life Care' was written at the top of the front page in green letters. My mouth twisted with rage. I snatched the leaflet and stood up, signalling to Ben that it was time for us to leave.

'Thank you, Dr Newman,' I said firmly, before spinning on my heel and making a beeline for the door. We hurried downstairs, out of the exit and into the back of a taxi towards home.

'I don't want to do it.' I turned to him in the seat next to me, slapping my hands against my thighs in indignation. 'I don't want to get married just for the sake of it. Out of fear!' *How dare she?* And anyway, in my mind and heart we were already married and then some. We'd navigated more highs and lows together than relationships I knew of that had spanned decades. We'd travelled the world, from the Nevada Desert and the Yucatan jungle to Northern Africa and the Western Ghats. We'd lived in half a dozen different homes, endured long distances between us, danced at countless festivals and negotiated massive career changes. We'd welcomed little ones to our families and celebrated marriages. I'd lost grandparents. He'd lost a half-brother and his dad. His illness had only made our love and devotion for each other grow. Never mind that Dr Newman was an expert, who had dedicated her life to treating this particular type of cancer. She was wrong, I insisted. *She was categorically wrong!* I shook my head, as if to shake her words right out of it. He would heal, and we would have our dream wedding in Ibiza as planned. Besides, she hadn't explicitly said the d-word to us. So long as he was still breathing, there was hope.

For the next seventy-two hours, I propped myself up at the dining table with a pile of cushions and countless cups of coffee, trawling through the internet in a desperate search for a solution. There *had* to be something, I pleaded. We weren't giving up, not now. I was stirred up, crazed almost, fuelled by caffeine and adrenaline and love. Oh, the *love* . . . There was nothing I wouldn't do for that man, I thought to myself as I scoured every last corner of cyberspace. I would sail to the ends of the earth and back again a thousand times over. Somebody would have to *kill* me before I let him die.

Finally, in the dead of night three days later, I stumbled across the website of an alternative cancer treatment centre in Tijuana. I'd never heard of it before. According to Google, it was a city on the US–Mexico border just south of San Diego. It was deemed one of the most dangerous cities in the world, with murder rates among the highest in Mexico. *Shit*, I thought. Cancer, Covid *and* cartels. But the testimonials were too compelling to ignore. I sat up straighter, my eyes widening with disbelief as I read through each of them. Patients had arrived at the centre, with rare and aggressive late-stage cancers like Ben, and were walking out only weeks later completely cancer free. I was stunned.

The following morning, I helped him slip into his dressing gown and onto the sofa.

'I think I've found the answer,' I told him as I set down a cup of green tea and the morning's medicines on the table beside him. I explained what I'd read about the centre and the kinds of patients they treated there. I'd worked out that we had enough money left over from the fundraising drive for a few months' worth of treatment. We risked exposing ourselves to the virus by travelling, but his disease posed the greatest, most immediate, threat to his life.

'Let's do it,' Ben nodded, after watching the video testimonials with me for the dozenth time. 'But maybe we could go in a month or so, babe? I have nothing left to give right now. I need some time to heal. I need to build up my strength again.'

'Benny,' I said gently, turning to him. 'I'm not sure we can delay this by a month. If we're going to go, we need to go as soon as possible. We don't have the luxury of time.'

His eyes narrowed and his brow pulled downwards in a frown.

'Okay,' he answered quietly, after a while. 'But first, I really need a holiday.'

Later that afternoon, I booked us two one-way flights to Ibiza, leaving the following week. Jean, Christiaan and Nicole would join us for a few days so the five of us could spend some quality time together. From there, Ben and I would fly on to Tijuana via Mexico City for treatment, and they would fly home. We organised a telephone consultation with the medical team at the centre for the end of the week, and enrolled him in the programme. I cleaned the flat, washed our laundry and packed our bags.

As the plane descended over the Balearic Sea towards the runway in Ibiza, tears rolled down my face. We'd dreamed of this day for months, and to be honest, some days I thought it might never come. In the face of a global pandemic, lockdown and stage-four cancer, it seemed nigh on impossible that we'd ever get here. I could feel the edges of my body soften the moment the wheels touched the ground.

We picked up our hire car outside the terminal and set up shop by the pool at Casa Maca for the afternoon, our favourite hotel hidden away in the hills of Can Palau just outside of Ibiza's old town. The owners – Ben's clients, Christian and Alan – had renovated the eighteenth-century farmhouse a few years earlier, and had invited us to stay while it was still under construction back in 2018. They'd preserved the farmhouse's traditional Ibicencan features throughout, like the oil mill that stood in the main lobby, and the native almond, fig, and olive trees in the gardens. Every trip to Ibiza since had called for a visit to the open-air restaurant that overlooked the ancient fortress of Dalt Vila and the Mediterranean Sea. Sitting under the stars, eating fresh food grown onsite, was nothing short of magical.

'I feel like I've done more healing in the last hour than I've done in the last seven months,' Ben said, grinning at me from behind his prawn taco. Lime juice dripped down his fingers as he took another bite. I threw a napkin into his lap and smiled back at him. I felt the same. To be back in our happy place, the place we'd dreamed of getting married in and calling home one day, was a balm for my battered soul.

After we finished lunch, we drove through the island's interior along the winding country lanes to Cala D'Hort, a beach in the south-west corner of the island. Out of all the beautiful beaches the island had to offer, it was without doubt my favourite. The air whipped across my skin and through my hair, infused with the scent of salt and pine. I reached over to Ben and rested my hand on the back of his head, his skin hairless and smooth. He smiled at me, the kind of smile I hadn't seen in months: one of pure joy. Turning right onto the road that led down to the beach, a line of brilliant blue suddenly appeared on the horizon, punctured by the top of a towering limestone formation. The approach to the beach had never ceased to take my breath away in all the years we'd visited. The formation, known as Es Vedrà, was said to be home to the sirens and sea nymphs who lured Odysseus, the legendary Greek king of Ithaca, from his ship in Homer's poem, *The Odyssey*. We parked the car and headed down the road towards the beach, bags and towels in hand. After a minute or so, the white cliffs came into view. At the bottom of the cliffs stood a cluster of traditional fishermen's huts, *casetas varadero*. We laid our towels down on the sand and got undressed.

'I'm going for a swim,' Ben said, the smile still painted across his face. It would be the first time he'd submerged himself underwater in over three months; the PICC line, a type of catheter inserted into his arm ahead of chemo through which the drug would be administered, hadn't been allowed to get wet in case of infection. I watched as he walked towards the shore, into the water, before sinking his body beneath the surface. *His beautiful, broken body*, I thought. I lay down and dug my arms and legs into the sand under my towel. I closed my eyes, letting my thoughts drift to the days spent on the back of his moped, chasing music across the island, when we were young and in love without a care in the world. Back then, our only concern had been which nightclub to attend. I longed for those days. Life had felt so much simpler. *They're coming*, I insisted. Better days were coming.

Later that afternoon, we drove back to the airport to pick up Jean, Christiaan and Nicole. We hugged each other tightly, each of us sensing the relief of escaping reality, if only in our minds and for a brief moment in time. We checked them in to the hotel and freshened up, before heading west to a restaurant tucked away between the coves of Cala Gracio and Punta Galera for dinner. Perched on the edge of the cliff, surrounded by lush fauna and flora, the restaurant was home to one of the best sunsets on the island. The sun, a molten orb, hung low on the horizon as we descended the pathway towards the entrance, the sky painted in hues of gold and fiery red. We ordered a glass of wine each, a basket of bread, blue cheese croquettes and burrata for starters. Then, out came sea bass fillets roasted in garlic and white wine, watermelon salad, French fries and padron peppers for mains. After months of misery, it was only right that Ben should indulge.

'Cheers!' he said, raising his glass. 'Here's to a bright future ahead – for all of us.'

I beamed at him as we clinked glasses. We needed this: a moment to feel normal again, to return to the time before, where different versions of ourselves lived a different version of our lives before cancer came along.

A few days later, we said goodbye to his family at Ibiza airport, and began our journey to Tijuana. It would take us around two days to get there, with a transfer at London Heathrow and a night's stop-over in Mexico's capital. Ben was too weak to travel all that way without assistance, and he was transferred on and off the planes and through the airports in a wheelchair. The sight shook me to my core. I knew he was ill, but I didn't know how ill – or rather, I didn't want to know. At home, in isolation, it had been easier to remain in denial. I'd dismissed his need to sleep all day as a side effect of the chemo. In Ibiza, spirits had been high. At no point did I ever think – did I ever *allow* myself to think, even – that maybe, he was approaching the beginning of the end. Now, surrounded by people who didn't have cancer, it dawned on me just how ill he actually was. I wondered how he must have felt. Was he feeling self-conscious? Embarrassed? At this point, did he even care? A voice over the tannoy invited passengers with special assistance to board first. Dozens of eyes bored into us as we joined the front of the queue to board, pity stretched across each face. I wanted to throw myself over him, to protect him. I wanted to scream at them, 'He's *not* going to die!'

After eventually landing in Tijuana, we took a taxi to our hotel, which was located next door to the treatment centre in the city's business district, Zona Rio. A heat haze shimmered above the asphalt as we crawled along the motorway in gridlocked traffic, sandwiched between enormous pickup trucks with blacked-out windows. I squeezed Ben's hand, trying hard to block out the statistics I'd read online about human trafficking and cartel violence as the car crept towards our destination. Our relief was palpable as we pulled up outside. We took the escalators towards the lobby and checked in at reception, after which a member of staff showed us to our room on the sixth floor. We could see the border wall in the distance from our window, an ugly, grey monolith bursting out of the scorched brown earth. The room hardly felt like a home away from home – with harsh, sterile lighting, stiff grey bed sheets and neon orange curtains – but it didn't matter. We were here for one reason, and one reason only: to save Ben's life. We put our bags down, drew the curtains, and collapsed into bed.

The next day, we headed across the road to the centre for Ben's first consultation with the medical team. Vases of pink dahlias were dotted around the reception area. A dozen or so positive quotes were splashed across the walls painted in a warm cornflower blue. The air swelled with a sense of hope that had eluded us until now.

We sat down on the sofa opposite the reception desk, when a stout, sweet-looking lady suddenly appeared. She handed Ben a form to fill out before leading us down the corridor towards Dr

Bernardo's office. Dr Bernardo, she informed us, was the head doctor at the centre, and would be overseeing Ben's treatment while he was there.

'Welcome,' he said as we stepped through the door, his smile emanating warmth. He handed us a folder outlining Ben's treatment schedule for the next three weeks. Ben would be at the centre for six hours a day, six days a week, receiving all sorts of different treatments – from HALO therapy, full body hyperthermia, rife machine therapy, mag ray, pulsed electromagnetic field therapy to radiofrequency ablation and sonodynamic therapy, as well as vitamin and mineral IVs. The list went on and on.

'We've successfully treated patients in similar situations to you before, Ben,' Dr Bernardo said, sensing our overwhelm. Finally, a doctor believed what we believed: that he could heal.

Before long, we adjusted to a new rhythm. While Ben was in treatment, I sat in the waiting area and pored over books I'd brought from England by Dr Joe Dispenza, a scientist and researcher said to have healed compressed vertebrae in his spine with just his mind, following a serious cycling accident that almost left him paralysed. Each of his books explained that, by harnessing the power of our minds, we could change matter, like cancer cells, in the quantum field. According to Dr Dispenza, the quantum field was an invisible field of energy and information – or a field of intelligence or consciousness – that existed beyond space and time. I wrote reels of notes, folded pages, highlighted and underscored the lines. Occasionally, I stepped outside and took a walk around the block. I plotted out our travel itinerary once treatment was over: we'd head west to Oaxaca to celebrate his remission, and then to Quintana

Roo and Yucatan. The days wore on, each one indistinguishable from the last.

By the end of the third week, a quiet optimism was beginning to rise inside of me. *Maybe it's working*, I thought as I sat across from Ben in the canteen at the centre one evening. I'd noticed the colour returning to his cheeks and his hair was regrowing. He was eating more and steadily putting on weight. He had even begun joining me on my daily walks, walking a bit further each time. He stood taller, his spine straighter, shoulders back. There was a new spring in his step, each stride longer and easier than the last. But then again, neither of us had had even the faintest clue that cancer had been steadily engulfing his lungs for three whole months prior to the terminal diagnosis back in March. And that was what made this disease so insidious, I thought, as I watched him knock back his second protein smoothie and smack his lips. I almost didn't want to know, the thought of it *not* working too terrifying to entertain. If it hadn't, it only meant one thing.

On Tuesday 6th October, a month or so into the programme, we walked back into Dr Bernardo's office to find out. As we sat down in the chairs opposite him, I could barely breathe, anxiety tightening its grip around my chest.

'I've got good news for you,' he smiled. Ben and I looked at each other cautiously. 'The disease is stable.' He turned his computer around to reveal an outline of Ben's torso, with blobs of white and clouds of grey in different shapes dotted throughout. 'If you look here,' he said, 'some of the tumours are the same size, some are smaller, and some have even disappeared altogether.'

'Oh my God,' I cried, leaping out of my seat. 'Yes! YES! I bloody knew it – I knew it!' I fist-pumped the air and turned to look at Ben.

'Wow,' he uttered quietly, goggle-eyed in disbelief.

Euphoria surged through my body. I collapsed into my seat as tears poured down my cheeks. For seven months, doors had been continually slammed shut. Things we'd pinned all of our hopes on had amounted to nothing. Doctors had told us no. But now? He was actually doing it: he was defying the odds and healing.

'Since the treatment is working well,' Dr Bernardo continued, 'I suggest you book onto the programme for another month, by which point we can assess your progress again and decide where to go from there. How does that sound?'

'Yes. Yes, absolutely,' said Ben. 'Let's do it. Thank you so much, Dr Bernardo. I'm so grateful for your help.' He gulped down a sob. We thanked him again and stumbled back into the waiting area, where we recorded a video to share with our families.

'I can't believe I'm telling you this,' Ben wept into the camera. 'I never thought I'd get to say it. It's working. The treatment is actually working.'

11

The following week, 16th October 2020, marked our six-year anniversary. We sat in a private room at the centre after a day of treatment, eating falafel, hummus and tabbouleh out of polystyrene boxes from a Lebanese restaurant down the road. Ben had developed a cough a few days before, and Dr Bernardo had suggested he stay in for the night so the staff could monitor him.

'It's probably just the dead cancer tissue in your lungs,' he'd reassured us. 'Take a couple of days off treatment, see how you get on.' His deduction sounded plausible enough. I guess the tissue had to go somewhere.

'Don't worry about it,' I told him. 'I promise you next year's going to look different. Maybe we could even go back to Amsterdam again, where it all started.'

'I'd love that,' he wheezed.

It wasn't quite how either of us had expected to celebrate it, but if the past fifteen months had taught us anything, it was that nothing was guaranteed. And anyway, I couldn't have cared less where we were or what we were doing, so long as we spent it together.

◆ ◆ ◆

Over the next couple of days, I tried to quell my growing suspicion that something wasn't right. What had started as a mild cough the week before was now rattling and violent. I'd watch, in a panic, as he'd descend into a coughing fit in our hotel room, clutching at his chest. On 20th October, I walked him back to the treatment centre, demanding that the doctors run some tests on him. They advised him to stay overnight again.

'I don't want to be alone,' he said to me that evening as he sat on his hospital bed. He was tracing his fingers along his sternum. He'd made a habit of doing that lately, telling me he was 'just feeling for things'. *But what things?* I often wondered. Could he actually feel the cancer? Was he in pain?

'Then you won't be, my love,' I soothed. 'We'll have a sleepover and make it fun.'

The oxygen tank next to his bed whirred. I kissed him on the forehead and then kissed his cheeks. He coughed and winced, pushing the prongs of his nasal cannula into his nostrils. I had tucked the tubes behind his ears and was pulling the strap of his oxygen mask over the back of his head, when Dr Bernardo suddenly appeared in the doorway.

'I'm leaving now,' he told us. 'The doctors who are doing the night shift will be round shortly. Is everything okay?'

'Yes,' I nodded meekly. But how would I know if it wasn't? What signs were I supposed to be looking out for? Wasn't Dr Bernardo meant to tell me if everything was okay? The responsibility petrified me. He waved goodbye and disappeared round the door again. I lifted the head of the bed to elevate Ben's upper body and propped his pillows up behind his back. 'Close your eyes,' I told him softly. I pulled my chair up next to his bed and stroked his head. 'There's nothing to fear, my love. Slow, gentle, easy breaths. Remember: I am healthy, I am healed. I am whole.'

For the rest of the night, I sat in the chair teetering on the edge of sleep, jolted awake, heart racing, every time he coughed or cleared his throat again. I adjusted his face mask as he shuddered and twitched, and checked the number on the oximeter attached to his index finger. His blood oxygen level was hovering between ninety-four and ninety-five. I typed it into Google. Apparently, a value between ninety-five and one hundred was considered normal for healthy individuals. *Everything's fine, everything's fine, everything's fine*, I tried to convince myself, as I had done countless times in recent months.

By the time the sun broke through the nylon curtains hours later, I woke to find Ben saturated in sweat. He blinked open his eyes, his chest heaving, each breath even more shallow and quick than the one before. He looked at me and forced a smile, before swinging his legs over the side of the bed. Steadying himself against the headboard, he pushed himself up to his feet and fell backwards. *CRACK!*

'What was that?!' I shrieked. I leapt out of my chair and seized both of his shoulders.

Alarm flashed across his eyes. 'My chest,' he panted. 'It came fro— from my chest!'

'Okay, it's okay. You're okay, baby. Stay sitting down. Try to focus on your breath, okay? I'll go get a doctor, don't worry.' I sprinted out of the room and turned left down the corridor towards reception. Dr Bernardo was standing by the front desk with a clipboard in his hands. 'Excuse me, Dr Bernardo, sorry to interrupt you. Please can you come and check on Ben? I'm worried. Something's not right.'

He followed me into the room and checked the oximeter still attached to Ben's finger. The number had dropped to eighty-nine. His brow furrowed with concern.

'What's happening?' My voice trembled.

Another doctor entered the room. They talked hurriedly to one another in Spanish and I attempted to grasp on to the few words that I understood. *Urgencia . . . Paramédicos . . .* I darted back and forth between the two of them. 'Will somebody please tell me what's going on?'

Dr Bernardo turned to me. 'Ben needs urgent medical attention and we can't give it to him here. We're calling the local hospital to send an ambulance for him.'

An ambulance? What on earth did he need an ambulance for? And weren't they doctors?! *Why the fuck couldn't they treat him here?* I looked at Ben, still gasping for breath. The number on his oximeter was plummeting. Eighty-seven. Eighty-four, then eighty.

'It's okay, baby,' I whimpered, desperation clinging to my vocal cords. 'You're going to be okay. Just breathe. Nice and steady, in and out.'

Time seemed to slow down. Voices drawled, vowels drawn out. *Focus, Lotte,* I told myself. The floor started spinning, the air thin and compressed. *Focus. Don't lose it now . . .*

The door to his room flew open all of a sudden. I sprung to my feet and looked on, paralysed by terror, as three paramedics burst into the room wheeling a gurney.

'Payment,' demanded one of them, thrusting a card machine into my face. 'Ten thousand dollars. You need to make payment before we take him.'

Shit! There was no time to think. I needed to act, and fast. I reached into Ben's pocket and pulled out his wallet. I jammed his card into the machine and punched in the PIN as the paramedics lifted him onto the gurney and strapped him down.

'*¡Vamos!*' one of them yelled.

I ran behind them as they raced through the corridor, into the lift, down three floors, and into the back of the ambulance parked up outside. I heaved open the passenger door and threw myself onto the seat next to the driver. My heart pounded, a drumroll of panic inside my chest. The sirens blared as we tore down the road and joined the stream of traffic on the motorway. I clung on to the grab handle as we lurched from left to right, dodging in and out of the string of vehicles. The seconds felt like minutes, the minutes like hours, when eventually the ambulance pulled up to the entrance to A&E. The back doors swung open. Out came the gurney, Ben sitting upright gasping. The paramedics rushed him towards the entrance. I tried to follow them, but a burly security guard stepped out in front of me.

'No, no, no,' he said, shaking his hands in my face. '*No puedes entrar.*'

What?!

'LOTTE!' Ben shouted after me, his eyes wide with terror. The oximeter on his finger was flashing 'LOW' in red.

'It's okay, my love!' I cried after him. 'I'm coming, I'm coming!'

He disappeared behind the folding doors and a swarm of people closed in on me speaking in Spanish. '*Mi novio,*' I cried. '*No comprendo. ¡Mi novio!*' I fumbled for my phone in my pocket and staggered towards the foldout chairs that lined the entrance, before falling into the dust on all fours. Steadying myself against the chair leg with one hand, I dialled my siblings back in England.

'Guys,' I sobbed. 'Oh my God, I don't know what's happened, I . . . I think Ben's going to die!'

'Sis, it's okay,' said Oliver on the other end of the phone. 'Calm down. Where are you? Tell us where you are first!'

'I don't know,' I choked. 'I . . . I'm at a hospital.' I looked up and scanned the sign next to the entrance. It said 'CRUZ ROJA' in big red letters. 'The Red Cross, I think. He's been coughing, and then last night— I don't know. It suddenly got so much worse. I don't know what to do,' I wailed. 'I don't even know where I am!'

'Darling,' said Georgia. 'It's okay. We're here. Are you sitting down? Try to find somewhere to sit down. It's okay. Breathe.'

'Excuse me,' came a voice suddenly. 'Are you Benjamin's partner?' The accent was thick like glue. I looked up to find a doctor standing beside me.

'Yes,' I whimpered. 'That's me.'

'Hi,' said the man. 'My name is Dr Vargas. Is it okay if we talk for a moment?'

I nodded and climbed to my feet, phone in hand.

'Guys, a doctor is here and he wants to talk to me. I'll have to call you back.' I hung up the phone and staggered behind him through the entrance to the hospital and into a waiting room inside.

'Please, take a seat,' he offered, handing me a PPE mask and goggles. 'I'm one of the intensivists in the Covid intensive care unit. The cancer centre called to tell us about the situation that happened there this morning. I need you to understand that Benjamin is very critical right now.'

I heaved.

'But look, we're going to do our best to stabilise him. Here.' He passed me a small plastic cup filled with water. 'Have a drink.'

I nodded again.

'We're going to put him on a mechanical ventilator to help him breathe. Can I ask . . . Do you know if either of you have been exposed to Covid-19 recently?'

'No,' I gulped, shaking my head. At least, I didn't think we had been exposed to it. Ben had a cough, yes – and I had a sore throat, but we could still smell and taste everything. The latest published information stated that loss of smell and taste were the two key symptoms to look out for. I'd thought nothing of it. We were safe inside the treatment centre. And besides, the doctors there hadn't mentioned anything about Covid.

'Okay. Well, I'm going to need you to take a test anyway, but we can't do it for you here. You'll need to go to a lab. Once you've done it, you'll have to go back to your hotel and quarantine while you wait for the results. Would you like to see him before you go?'

He led me back through the corridor towards the entrance to the intensive care unit. I gasped as I caught sight of Ben lying naked under a chequered sheet on a gurney surrounded by doctors in hazmat suits, goggles and masks. He was out cold, mouth wide open as one of them squeezed the air from a bag valve mask into his lungs.

'It's okay, my love,' I told him as I stroked the top of his head, tears falling into my goggles and blurring the glass. 'You're going to be okay. I promise.'

Still shaking, I blundered back outside and typed in the address of the lab into the Uber app on my phone. Where was I? I kept wondering as the driver navigated a series of deserted side roads. I traced the black line on the map, panic-stricken. I had never ventured this far from the treatment centre before. I hadn't told anyone back home where I was going. *Hold steady, Lotte!*

After twenty or so minutes, the car pulled up to a lab at the end of a quiet street in a rundown neighbourhood seconds away from the border wall. I breathed a sigh of relief as I climbed out of the car.

'I need a Covid test, please,' I squeaked to the man sitting behind the reception desk. He gestured towards a small, windowless room to my left.

'*¡Adelante, por favor!*' said a young woman appearing in the doorway. I sat down in the chair next to her while she prepared the swab.

'Tilt your head back for me, please,' she demanded. Before I knew it, she had jammed the swab deep inside my nostril. I yelled and threw my head backwards, hitting the wall, tears forming in my eyes. In went the second one, even deeper this time. 'All done.' She smiled sweetly. 'You can go now.'

I took another Uber back to the hotel and paced up and down the room, frantic. What the hell had happened back there? Could a tumour have exploded in his lungs? Had he caught the virus? I ran through all the possibilities in my head, none of which made any sense. How could everything have come undone so swiftly?

Hours later, Dr Vargas finally called me to confirm my worst fears: both of our Covid tests had come back positive. He explained that Ben had developed such a severe infection because of the cancer burden in his lungs, that it had led to acute pneumonia by the time he was admitted to hospital.

But how? I kept asking myself. *How did we catch it in the first place?* Symptoms, I read, could appear from anything between two to fourteen days after being exposed to the virus. I retraced my steps like a woman possessed. Back to the centre, to the hotel canteen. To the cafe across the road. Maybe it was me who caught it first. Maybe I'd passed it on to him. As night fell, my thoughts unravelled into a dark spiral of turmoil and guilt. Maybe it was all my fault.

12

Over the next few days, time seemed to fold in on itself. My symptoms quickly took hold of me. I lay in bed incapacitated, pain stabbing at my chest, lethargy soaking into my bones. The wait for the daily update from the hospital was a fresh kind of hell. Sometimes, I waited thirty-plus hours between calls. I tried to stay positive, to fill the time somehow. I stared at the TV hanging on the wall opposite my bed, catching the odd word in Spanish that I knew. I counted the four by fours on the motorway headed for the border from the window until I made myself feel sick. I ordered room service – a cheese omelette with a side serving of nachos and coriander garnish, *chilaquiles verdes* on repeat. I figured it would take me ten minutes to finish each meal, maybe fifteen if I really took my time with every bite. I posted updates about Ben's condition to social media and GoFundMe, continuing to raise funds to cover the hospital fees that were exceeding thousands of dollars each day. I spoke to people on Instagram and FaceTimed my family and friends. I wrote diary entries and meditated, delusions of magical thinking growing stronger by the minute. 'If I write another entry, if I meditate a bit more, he'll heal.' I was sure of it. On the seventh day since his admission, Dr Vargas called me, Jean, Christiaan and Nicole with a glimmer of hope.

'If everything goes to plan, we'll take Ben off the ventilator at some point this week. He keeps trying to wake up. We're in the unit with him now, and we think he's aware enough to hear us. Would you like to speak to him?'

'Oh my God,' his family and I replied in unison. 'Yes. Please!'

He put the camera on and turned his phone around. Ben was lying in the bed in a hospital gown, comatose, with several tubes hanging from his mouth.

'Oh, Benny,' I uttered, gawping at my phone in horror. I wanted to reach through the screen and hold him, kiss him – *something*.

'Hi, Benny,' the four of us exclaimed.

Slowly but surely, he turned his head as if to follow the sound of our voices. My heart leaped as his left eye opened a sliver.

'Benny!' I cried. 'You're okay, my love. You're in safe hands.'

For the next ten minutes, we told him how much we loved him, how strong he had been, how amazing we thought he was. We told him about all the fundraising efforts from countless people all over the world. I watched as his pixelated head moved about. Was he trying to tell us something? I wondered. Was he feeling distressed?

'We're going to get you home. We promise.'

We told him we loved him one more time and hung up the call. I slumped backwards onto the bed and lay there for a while, completely overcome. My emotions eddied, a mixture of elation and fear and relief. Ben was conscious. Very sedated, granted – and clearly very sick – but conscious nonetheless. And that was more than we'd had all week. I tried to imagine what it felt like to be in his position, to see through his eyes. Did he have a notion of where he was and what was happening? What must it have felt like to hear us, and not be able to talk?

The following morning, I sat up in bed and grabbed my phone to find an email notification from an American oncologist based in

Beverly Hills called Dr Christie. We'd had a private online consultation with him months earlier – it was he who had suggested we test the tumour samples in case Ben was eligible for immunotherapy.

'EUREKA!' he wrote. 'I just received the news that a new form of RNA-enrichment was developed and your tumour sample was re-tested. It shows an NTRK1 fusion. This is the best news as there is a drug called larotrectinib that typically has a one hundred per cent remission rate in NTRK+ cancers. Please contact your oncologist in the UK immediately to order this drug. And congratulations!'

I stared at the email in disbelief. The quality of Ben's tumour tissue was so degraded by the time it had arrived at the laboratory for testing, that the first and second rounds of testing earlier in the summer had yielded no results. The lab had spent the last few months developing their technology and had tested it again. I read his email ten more times just to be sure. There was a cure. *A cure!* But we were in Tijuana . . . *How would we get our hands on it?* And just to complicate matters more, Ben was unconscious. On life support. *Even if we could get hold of it, how was he supposed to even take it?* My head spun. In any normal circumstances, he would need to sign waivers and agree to receiving the treatment. But this was anything but normal – if there was ever a time that called for bending the rules, this was it. I forwarded the email to Ben's family back in Europe and asked them to call me as soon as they could.

By day fourteen, I was out of quarantine. Christiaan and Nicole flew over from England for a few days in the hope that they would be around for when Ben was taken off the ventilator. Dr Christie fought tooth and nail to get hold of the drug in LA from the pharmaceutical giant Bayer. Once they'd given us the green light, a plan was formed: a friend of Ben's who was based in LA would collect the drug from Dr Christie's pharmacy in Beverly Hills, drive it down to San Diego and hand it to a friend of a friend, a Mexican citizen, who would bring it across the border into Tijuana and deliver it to me in a few days' time. In the meantime, Christiaan, Nicole and I were granted permission to visit Ben in the intensive care unit, so long as we dressed head to toe in protective gear.

The unit was as every bit as shocking as I'd imagined it to be. Doctors in gas masks wandered between windowless rooms where patients lay half dead on ventilators. We stuck the photos Nicole had printed on the wall opposite Ben's bed – photos of his mum and dad, photos of us on the beach in southern Spain, photos from his jiu jitsu grading ceremony back in 2019. He'd see them once he was awake, we thought. It would give him something to look forward to, to work towards. We left a speaker on the table in the corner of the room, playing hours of his favourite songs on loop. We tried to stay positive, but by the time Christiaan and Nicole left, Ben was still on the ventilator, and instead of getting better, the extent of his complications was steadily growing. He had sepsis, hypoxemia, influenza, acinetobacter, and acidosis, along with a whole host of other complications I hadn't managed to catch the name of. I tried to keep myself busy and useful between Dr Vargas's calls. I wrote social media updates and press releases in the hope of spreading the word about Ben's situation and raising more funds for treatment. I invited my friends, family and followers on social media to join me in group meditations on Zoom every night. 'Visualise his body healed and well,' I asked the participants. 'This version of him already exists as a possibility in the quantum field.'

Finally, on 11th November, the drug was administered through Ben's nasogastric tube.

'Now, we just have to wait and see what happens,' Dr Vargas told us with a half smile.

◆ ◆ ◆

The next couple of days blurred together. One of my best friends who I met on the first day of secondary school, Jaz, had flown in from England to keep me company. 'Talk to me about your wedding day,' she'd say to me, trying her hardest to stop me from drowning in despair. 'I can't *wait*. What sort of dress are you thinking you'll wear?'

I already knew the answer to this, obviously. I'd already picked the damn dress – off-white, spaghetti straps, backless, tight. A hundred and sixty quid from a boutique brand online. I pulled a photo of the dress up on my phone and showed it to her.

'Corrr, yeah, I love it!' she exclaimed. She had a kind of resolve and optimism like no one else. In times of crises, there weren't many other people I'd have wanted by my side. As a refugee rights advocate focusing on amplifying stories of displacement, she'd helped countless people over the years. Her empathy was inexhaustible, it seemed. Normally I'd have soaked every last bit of her up, marinated in her energy, just as I had done for the last nineteen years – but now it bumped against me, my mind fixated on Ben.

Three days later, on the 14th November, we sat down in one of the cafes a few blocks from the hotel to order some food, when my phone rang. Dr Vargas was video calling.

'*Fuck*,' I mouthed, stopping dead in my tracks.

'Hello?'

Dr Vargas's face suddenly appeared on my screen, along with Jean, Christiaan and Nicole's. 'Lotte,' he said gravely. 'I suggest you come to the hospital as soon as you can.' The expression on his face revealed what he was going to say before the words had even left his mouth. My blood ran cold. *No!* 'I'm so sorry, but Ben is about to pass away.'

I turned to Jaz. 'What's going on?' she asked me.

102

'We've got to go. He's dying. We need to leave, he's dy—'

I ran outside and steadied myself against the wall, Jaz not far behind me. The world had somehow tilted on its axis, the ground moving beneath my feet. I punched in the hospital's address into the Uber app. 'Your driver is five minutes away.'

'FUCK!' I screamed. The convulsions started, my limbs jerking this way and that.

I stared at the car on the app, all of the words and lines melting. *Faster! Come on!* Three minutes, then two. The seconds stretched out in front of me. I blinked, my vision blurring. *Why is everything upside down all of a sudden?* After what felt like hours, the taxi finally pulled up in front of the entrance to the cafe. Jaz wrenched the passenger door open and we jumped in.

'Stay calm,' she said, grabbing my hand. 'Just try to stay calm.'

'¡*Muy rápido!*' I begged the driver. If Ben was going to die, I wouldn't let him die alone. Not on my watch. No way. We swerved along the motorway, dodging the traffic. *Stay strong, Lotte. Don't fade into the darkness.*

Minutes later, my phone rang. It was Dr Vargas again.

'I'm so sorry,' he said quietly. 'Ben has just passed away.'

I choked out a feeble 'no' in protest as thousands of shards of blunt glass tore my heart from its cavity. 'I'm coming,' I gasped, 'I'll be there soon. I'm coming!' I needed to see him. I didn't care what he looked like, or what it would do to me. We needed to be together. *The agony. The agony. He can't be!*

We pushed through the doors to the entrance of A&E and staggered down the hallway towards the holding room that separated the Covid intensive care unit from the rest of the hospital. Inside, a nurse sprayed us down with disinfectant. She helped me into the plastic shoe covers and hazmat suit before turning to Jaz. I pulled on my mask, goggles and hair-net, and two layers of latex gloves, bound to my sleeves with Sellotape. I entered the ward, bewildered, Jaz beside me, the white sterile lights overhead searing into the back of my eyes. We stumbled towards Ben's door and caught sight of him lying lifeless under a chequered polyester sheet. A flat line ran across the monitor above him. I ran towards him and collapsed on top of the bed.

'No, no, no,' I howled. It wasn't real . . . *It can't be.* I lifted up the sheet and ran my gloves over his body, mottled yellow and purple. Pallor mortis . . . The urge to touch him one last time over-ruled my compliance with Covid regulations. The virus had already stolen so much from us. I needed to feel his hair, to press my lips against his skin.

'It's okay, darling,' came a voice that wasn't Jaz's. 'I'm right there with you.' *Who is that?*

I ripped off my gloves in defiance. I pulled his eyelids upwards, looking for a sign of life. Any sign . . .

Breathe.

Maybe Dr Vargas had got it wrong. Maybe the medical staff had made a mistake. That was it. This wasn't really happening . . .

But his eyes. His eyes . . . They weren't green anymore. He looked different . . . *Dead.*

'I love you,' I sputtered, hoping he could still hear me. What was that book? *The Tibetan Book of the Dead*? What had it said? That a dying person could still hear in the moments before and after death?

'I love you I love you I LOVE YOU!'

I lay there next to him for a while, time suspended. I pressed the palm of his hand against my face, knotted my fingers through his, smelled his skin. He didn't smell like him anymore – that famil-iar, comforting smell of home.

'I've had enough,' I whispered to Jaz some time later. 'There's no use in being here anymore.' She was sitting in the corner of the room, shaking. We pulled the photos down from the wall, packed up his speaker, and limped towards the door. *Don't look back, Lotte . . .*

'Moment by moment,' we whimpered, navigating our way through the corridors towards the exit. Moment by moment. *I must be dead too . . . Where are we? And my legs – where are my legs?*

Walking feels impossible, I thought. *Oh.* I stared at the floor with intense concentration, willing my feet to keep moving. Left, right, then left again. Each step carried me further away from him. Away from the life I'd tried so hard to salvage.

Black.

13

I don't know how we got home, or how we passed the time until the evening – chunks of time and memory ripped from me. I lay in bed as darkness fell, and a kind of madness ensued. I drifted in and out of sleep, tormented by images of his lifeless body and grey eyes. 'Where are you?' I cried as I thrashed about in agony, the shards of glass still buried under my skin, every last movement driving them deeper. What had they done with him? Was he in a body bag, in a refrigerator somewhere, reduced to a number on a tag? How could he have been here one minute, only to have disappeared in a puff of smoke the next? He was alive just yesterday. He was breathing – albeit mechanically – but he was *breathing*. None of it made any sense.

When daylight began to seep through the gap in the curtains, I rolled over and reached for my phone on the floor beside the bed. It was six o'clock in the morning, and Jaz was fast asleep next to me. The 'recent calls' page flashed up as I unlocked my screen. Annie was the last person I'd called. *When did I speak to Annie?* I wondered. I clicked on the 'Info' icon next to her name. 'I'm right there with you,' came her voice again in my mind. Seventeen minutes. I'd spoken to her for seventeen minutes in Ben's hospital room, and I hadn't remembered a thing besides those words.

I dragged my thumb upwards to the home screen. There were hundreds of notifications on WhatsApp and Instagram. *'NO,'* I gasped. A wave of dread flooded my body. England was seven hours ahead of Tijuana, and the news had spread throughout the day well before I'd hoped it would. A friend of Ben's had found out from Ben's family, and had already told his contacts in the music industry. *But it wasn't your news to share*, I thought to myself, scrolling through dozens and dozens of messages. I'd wanted to craft a statement of some kind. I'd wanted people to hear it from *me*, but only when I felt ready to share it, if at all. Maybe if I held off a bit longer, it would make it feel less real. Maybe I could even keep pretending that it *hadn't* happened, that it was just a nightmare I hadn't woken up from yet.

'I'm so sorry for your loss,' somebody wrote. I clicked through to the article they'd sent me from the BBC – 'UK Music Agent Ben Kouijzer Dies in Mexico Aged 36'.

'Jesus fucking Christ,' I cried. Why did they have to be so literal about it? Why couldn't they have written something less violent, like 'Ben Kouijzer Passes Away'? As if different wording would make it feel less final. As if there were varying degrees of dead.

'He was so loved,' wrote somebody else.

I heaved a loud 'fuck off' at my phone. Why the hell were they using past tense? He didn't belong in yesterday. My love hadn't stopped when his heart did – I *still* loved him.

My stomach made a loud rumbling noise, reminding me that the last time I'd eaten anything was over a day ago. Fuck food. Fuck everything. I wanted to lie there motionless for as long as possible, but the rumbles grew louder and louder. There were things my body required of me. I put my phone down on the bedside table and dragged myself to my feet. I gasped and clutched at the sides of my ribcage. There it was again, the agony . . .

My feet carried me in the direction of the bathroom, and I took off my clothes and stepped into the shower. His soap and cotton flannel stood on the ledge. I'd washed him in here only weeks ago, I thought to myself. How could he not need them anymore? I picked up the soap and flannel and carefully turned them over in my hands. I lifted the soap to my nose – notes of lavender and honey. *Mmm . . . just like his skin.* The flannel was stiff and crinkled. I pressed it against my eyes and cheeks. It softened and warmed as the water fell from the shower overhead. *This is the closest I'll get to him now.* What if I just draped it over my nose and mouth? Stood under the water for a bit, eventually stopped breathing? *No. Stop it.* I scanned the bathroom. His t-shirt was folded on the rail, his sandals by the door. This was all I had left of him, I thought to myself. *Inanimate objects . . .*

'Let's get some fresh air,' Jaz suggested as I emerged from the bathroom wrapped in my towel. I nodded. I needed her to make the decisions. We got dressed and took a taxi to Playa de Tijuana, a beach just south of the border wall. We walked along the boardwalk, arm in arm, watching in astonishment as the waves rolled in. Ben would never see the ocean again, I caught myself thinking. He'd never hear another birdsong, he'd never feel the sand beneath his feet.

'I'll have whatever you're having,' I said to Jaz as we sat down in the far corner of a restaurant – I stared at the menu in my hands, incapable of registering any of the words staring back at me. I could barely lift my head to meet the waiter's gaze, let alone undo the knots in my tongue. Every sound felt like an assault on my nervous system. The whooshing of the milk steamer, the clanging of crockery. The children laughing on the table next to us. The world kept spinning as if nothing had happened. How *dare* all these people go about their lives as normal, as if the greatest man to have ever lived hadn't just died? The sheer *audacity* of it. Didn't they know what I'd just lost? Couldn't they feel the white-hot agony engulfing my insides?

I couldn't leave the country without Ben, but global regulations prohibited the bodies of deceased patients who had died from Covid-19 or related causes to be repatriated to their home countries. His body would have to be cremated in Tijuana instead, and what was worse, the procedure would have to take place in adherence with Covid regulations – meaning nobody was allowed to attend. Business was clearly booming for the funeral industry, as the crematorium was booked up for the next week. I couldn't stand staying in Tijuana for a second longer, so I took a flight to San José Del Cabo, a coastal town two hours south, at the tip of Mexico's Baja California peninsula. My friend Jen flew out to swap places with Jaz who had to return home for work. Jen was a part of 'Team Disco' at CAA, and Ben's best friend in the office.

'I'm here for you,' Jen had messaged a few days earlier. 'Just tell me if you need me there, and I'll be on the next available flight.'

The hotel she had booked for us was reminiscent of a bygone era, all art deco and plush velvet inside. On the rooftop, a glass infinity pool overlooked the Sea of Cortés. I'd hoped that a change of scenery might take my mind off things, but three words kept ringing loudly in my head: 'Ben is dead, Ben is dead, Ben is dead.'

For the next few days, my body carried me through each minute and hour on autopilot. Jen stopped me from coming completely undone. She shared stories about Ben that I hadn't heard before, and encouraged my ideas to honour his memory, like setting up a music charity in his name and helping others navigate grief. On the day of the cremation, we walked to a thin stretch of beach near the hotel together and wandered along the sandbank in silence. I felt bone tired, as if I were dragging my body through treacle. I stopped occasionally, bending to pull a few leaves, frangipani, and grass from piles of dried seaweed, before binding them all together with a piece of driftwood. *Ben deserves so much more than this,* I thought to myself. It looked so puny and pathetic for a funeral spray.

Five minutes before the cremation, Jen and I parted ways, her heading towards one end of the beach and me towards the other. The moment felt so big and overwhelming that I couldn't bear to be around anyone. I needed to be alone, to let my grief spill out of me without worrying about how it would make her feel to witness it. I walked towards the edge of the water and stood there for a while, watching the waves roll in and retreat again. Bringing his body home had been the only consolation his family and I were holding out for. The virus had forced him to spend the last eight months of his life in isolation. It had rendered him incapable of breathing, and had left him to die alone. And now this? After everything he'd been through he deserved the dignity of returning to his family, and even that was taken from us. I ought to have been there in that room with him – *someone* ought to have been there at the very least.

At three o'clock, I released the driftwood into the water, watching the waves carry it further out to sea. I crouched down and closed my eyes, trying my hardest to hold a picture of him in my mind. His face kept coming and going, fading in and out. The man I had loved for six beautiful years had disintegrated into dust. Now, he was just a memory that flashed and flickered, like a TV screen disrupted by a weak signal.

On Monday 30th November, sixteen days after his death, we were finally able to leave Mexico. The journey back to London would require a transfer at Mexico City airport, and would take around thirty-four hours in total. My body was broken. I couldn't do it all without stopping. Instead, I needed to do it in stages – fly, then stop. Sleep, recuperate, then fly again. A few hours before the flight, we drove to the funeral home in downtown Tijuana to collect the urn.

'*Hola*,' said a gentleman from behind the desk as I walked inside. He offered me a commiserating smile as I passed him the death certificate. A brown jacket hung loosely from his shoulders, his lithe frame like a coat hanger inside it as he glided towards the curtain at the back of the room. He disappeared behind it for a few minutes, before reappearing with a velvet drawstring bag in his hands.

'*Muchas gracias*,' I uttered as I took the bag from him. '*Adiós*.'

I climbed into the back of the taxi and strapped the bag into the middle seat between me and Jen. We looked at each other, speechless. No words could possibly have offered even the smallest hint of comfort or sense. Instead, she reached over to me and squeezed my hand. I pulled my phone from my bag and looked up how to travel with cremated ashes. *You're still teaching me things, aren't you, babe?* I thought to myself. Of all the things I'd googled over the years, this was by far the strangest. To say I was feeling uneasy about transporting a box of white powder through and out of Mexico, a country notorious for drug-trafficking across borders, would be an understatement. Did I have the right documents? I needed several copies of the death certificate, the certificate of cremation, and the attestation form from the crematorium – a document that stated the urn contained the remains of Ben's ashes and nobody else's – in order to leave the country with them. The documents needed to be translated into both Spanish and English. Had I dotted all of the Is and crossed all of the Ts? In the grip of my shock and exhaustion, there was every possibility that I hadn't.

I pulled the urn out of the drawstring bag at airport security and lifted it onto the tray along with a small plastic bag of toiletries. I watched in disbelief as Ben, no taller than ten inches high and four inches wide, moved along the conveyor belt and through the X-ray machine. The cruel irony of it wasn't lost on me. Ever since his first diagnosis in July 2019, he'd become more and more concerned about anything and everything that was linked, no matter how loosely, to cancer. Everything that we'd ever shrugged off pre-diagnosis had suddenly posed a threat. The airport body scanners, he'd read, used a type of radiation to detect objects on or inside a person's body. He'd been desperate to mitigate the risks, even if it meant disclosing his diagnosis with security staff and opting for a heavy pat-down. I watched as the urn passed through to the other side and travelled along a different conveyor belt. *Shit,* I thought. I reached into my bag and pulled out the envelope containing the documents. A member of staff lifted the urn from the conveyor belt and beckoned me over. *Shit, shit, shit.* Over the last eight months, everything that could have possibly gone wrong had gone wrong, so why wouldn't this? My thoughts were running riot – to the security staff calling me into a private room, sifting through Ben with a drug detector, and probing my arsehole for baggies. Just my luck. I handed him the envelope with the documents inside and he leafed through them for a moment too long, before giving me a perfunctory nod and waving me through. 'Thank God,' I breathed.

Our hotel for the night was in Condesa, a trendy neighbourhood a thirty-minute taxi ride from Mexico City airport. With twenty-four hours to spare before the next flight, we dumped our bags in the room and headed out to explore with his ashes in tow. 'Ben will enjoy the sightseeing,' I said to Jen, as if he was, in fact, *in* the ashes somehow.

We walked past countless kerbside cafes and art nouveau mansions reminiscent of my year abroad in Paris during university. We wandered through the cedars, poplars and giant Montezuma cypress trees in Bosque de Chapultepec park, before heading to a restaurant in the Polanco neighbourhood. Pujol, I'd been told, was one of the best restaurants – if not *the* best restaurant in the whole of Mexico. Jen had made a reservation for lunch in an attempt to cheer me up. In any normal circumstances I'm sure I would have loved it, only nothing felt remotely normal now. Here I was, dining on baby corn skewered on top of a smoking pumpkin and dipped in ant mayonnaise, with Ben's remains in a rucksack under the table between my feet. I wondered what the staff would think if I told them. The courses kept coming – a two-thousand-day old *mole madre* complete with soft tortilla and a seasonal fruit sauce. A poached sea snail ceviche with heart of palm juice and parsnip purée. Lemon verbena custard with a swirl of yogurt frozen in liquid nitrogen. I swallowed down mouthful after mouthful, unable to really taste any of the flavours. Why should I get to enjoy any of this – to be alive even – when he wasn't?

The following evening, I walked through our departure gate at Mexico City airport, along the snaking corridor and onto the plane. I pushed the urn to the back of the overhead locker and collapsed into my seat beside Jen. Bits of me had already started to buckle and brace in anticipation of the onslaught of grief that I knew would hit me the moment I landed. I could feel it rumbling from the base of my spine, rearranging my organs. Over the last sixteen days, I'd tried to stuff it down, numb myself out in order to move through the motions of Mexican bureaucracy and tick off the two thousand things on my to-do-when-somebody-dies list. I wasn't dead like Ben was. I was still breathing – that much I was sure of – but I definitely didn't feel alive either. Like a mote of dust, I had slipped through the floorboards when his heart stopped, through the gap between two worlds – the land of the living and the land of the dead. There was no need to fight anymore, I thought, staring vacantly at the safety card tucked into the pouch in the seat in front of me. It was over – the appointments, the treatments, the hospitalisations. All the endless sleepless nights, the terror. It was all over. I checked the journey time – ten hours and thirty minutes. *Just hold on a bit longer,* I willed myself. Just ten hours and thirty minutes until I arrived home.

14

Mum and Dougal picked me up from Heathrow airport the next day. I couldn't bear to return to the flat in London, not yet. They drove me back to their house in Gloucestershire instead, where I'd be staying for the foreseeable. As soon as I slipped inside their front door three hours later, I crawled upstairs to the spare room and collapsed onto the bed.

'I feel like I'm dying, Mum,' I sobbed. Wretched, desperate sobs – the sort that demanded multiple ragged inhales in-between.

'Of course you do, darling,' Mum said, holding me. 'It's okay. Let it all out.' She felt my pain viscerally, the way I had felt Ben's. She knew she couldn't protect me. She knew she couldn't make it better, and I knew that crushed her. I could see it, tears pooling in her pale green eyes. Dougal sat quietly at the end of the bed, head dropped, a hand on Mum's shoulder. Apart from my siblings, they were the only two people I felt comfortable enough around to reveal the full force of my pain. Dad, on the other hand, had so far proved ineffectual.

'I don't know what to say,' he'd admitted over the phone the day he'd found out that Ben had died. It had rendered him completely lost for words, and I was furious.

'Something,' I wanted to reply. 'Anything!'

I pressed my face into the pillow and dug my nails into the duvet. My mouth contorted to make space for the screams. The noise. My God, the *noise*. I didn't think I was capable of making such a noise. It scared me. It was deranged, feral – like the mating call of a vixen on heat. What could be done though? I asked myself. Resistance was futile. The only thing I could do was to give myself over to it entirely. *Come on then*, I declared silently as I writhed about on top of the mattress. *Have your wicked way with me.* I lay there waiting for the sobs to subside for I don't know how long, until I was hollowed out like an empty husk.

My heart wasn't broken. *No*, I thought. This wasn't just a state of sadness. I'd have traded whatever this was for that, any day. After Dr Goulding had told us that Ben's cancer was terminal, I'd occasionally considered what it might feel like if he were to actually die. Nothing, absolutely nothing, could have prepared me for this. My grief, I decided, was best described as an all-consuming, unrelenting mind, body and soul experience. An annihilation of sorts, my skin torn at the seams, guts spilling out onto the floor. And it didn't let up – it followed me to the toilet, to the kitchen, to the sofa and back to bed again like a predator stalking its prey, waiting to rip its flesh clean off the bone. *I wasn't built to withstand such merciless pain*, I thought. It seemed to transcend even the boundaries of my own body. It unfurled and spiralled outwards, to the far edges of space. I was going to die, I was almost sure of it – and in all honesty, death had even begun to feel welcome. It was less that I actually wanted to kill myself – I hadn't exactly fleshed out the details, considered how and when as such – it was more that I wanted it all to go away. To just stop. Dying felt like the only thing that would grant me any respite.

Who was I without him? The question consumed me. His death had resulted in a complete dismantling of – no, a complete obliteration of – my sense of self. Over six beautiful years, my identity – my entire being, in fact – had become so deeply, so utterly, so inextricably woven into him. Into us. It was as if my brain had been wiped clean of the knowledge of what made me, me, and how I was supposed to go about, well, living. What was the point in living anymore, anyway? Wherever he was, that was home. That was where I wanted to be. There was a distinct lack of fucks to give about anything now that he was gone. His death had catalysed countless other losses. We'd never share another meal, or sit Botty to Botty on our sofa together. We'd never laugh at Steve Carrell in *The Office* on Netflix. We'd never get stuck inside a festival Portaloo, or get lost in music on a dance floor somewhere tropical. We'd never swim in another cenote, or drive along Route 395. We'd never have a wedding, or a child, or a villa in the Balearics. We'd never be retired together. We'd never have anything, ever again. It was loss on top of loss on top of loss. Grief on top of grief on top of grief. The future had looked so bright, so full of promise, but now it was as if I were stumbling down a deserted road to nowhere in the dead of night. An aching grief clung to me for things that were never really mine in the first place; fantasies of what could have been crumpled and burned like paper tossed to a flame.

I crawled into bed later that evening with his t-shirt. It was the last t-shirt he'd worn in Tijuana before he was admitted to ICU, and I hadn't washed it since. I nuzzled into it, a hint of him woven into the fabric still. I wedged myself between two pillows to buffer some of the pain, to feel something pressing against my body besides empty space. I hoped that maybe, just maybe, my heart would stop beating in my sleep. That it would save me doing the dirty work and let me slip away quietly without making a fuss. Insomnia quickly sunk its claws in as the light receded. I tossed and turned this way and that. Memories closed in – the trip we took last year, the last words I ever heard him speak. 'Lotte,' he'd cried.

'Lotte!' I studied the details of his face, the mole underneath his nostril, his eyes. His wide, terrified eyes . . . I searched the bed to feel the softness of his skin, the silk-like texture of his curls, only there was nothing – just two pillows and that empty space where his body ought to have been.

At last, I fell into a fitful sleep, only to wake again in the early hours. *Great*, I thought. *I'm alive. How bitterly disappointing.*

I lay there in that liminal space before daybreak, the silence broken by the first birdsong coming from somewhere nearby. *Is that Ben?* I wondered. *Good morning to you too, babe.* Maybe if I lay here for a bit longer, I thought to myself, I could pretend that it was all a dream.

I drifted through the next couple of weeks like an apparition moving in and out of the shadows. The normal rules of life were no longer applicable, not to me. My only job, right now, was to make it to the end of the day. Each one passed in a similar, listless fashion. I'd wake up, cry. Prop myself up in bed and sip the cup of lukewarm tea left for me on my bedside table. Follow the wafts of toast and coffee emanating from the kitchen downstairs. Push some breakfast around a plate, attempt to eat a few mouthfuls. Maybe have a shower and cry some more. Gaze out of the window. Convince myself that Ben had shape-shifted, that the dew drop blinking on a blade of glass in the garden was really him. Open another care package full of smellies, chocolates, herbal teas and jewellery sent by one of my friends, experience something alien inside my body that felt like momentary relief. Attempt to have a look at the probate spreadsheet Christiaan had created and tick off another task. Call another random number and inform another faceless stranger of his death. 'The acc— the account holder has d-died,' I'd stutter, struggling to organise the words in my mouth so they formed a coherent sentence. Repeat myself twice because they didn't hear me the first or second time. No condolences, just an 'I'll transfer you to the relevant department' delivered with a hint of boredom. Stare at the phone for a moment, outraged. Experience a flashback, which precedes a blow-by-blow replay of the events in question, to understand how and why the account holder is dead in the first place.

Each replay typically went a little something like this: I'd stagger into the living room and collapse onto the sofa next to Mum and Dougal, or text Mum and ask her to come to my bedroom urgently. She'd run in and cradle me as I wailed and thrashed about. Eventually she'd talk me back down, ground me. The incandescent pain would soften to an unrelenting sting. Together with Dougal, we'd pull three chairs up at the dining table and examine all of the correspondence relating to said events – rereading all the texts, WhatsApp threads, and emails, rehashing the dozen or so consultation recordings, and whatever memories of conversations I could salvage. I'd torment myself over all the if-onlys, what-ifs and maybes, and the two of them would soothe me, insist that it wasn't my fault. I'd give in and go back to bed to watch *RuPaul's Drag Race* on Netflix and numb out.

I'd nap. Wake up again. Sift through the internet and buy another jumper or bag or pair of shoes I didn't need in the hope that it might make me feel better (it didn't). Shuffle into the kitchen and weep into Mum's neck. Eat some spoonfuls of my favourite food that she'd lovingly prepared for me – wintry minestrone soup or shepherd's pie. Talk to Ben, who has now metamorphosed from dew drop to bird dancing on the kitchen window sill. Send some emails. Confirm the order of service and sandwich fillings for the funeral – cheese and pickle, and egg mayonnaise. Eat. Cry and eat again. Sit on the armchair next to Mum and Dougal, who are sitting on the sofa, and stare at the TV, unseeing. Go back to bed and sleep. Wrestle with nausea, insomnia, nightmares etcetera. Wake up. Rinse, repeat.

There was very little energy to do much else. Nobody warned me about the ramifications of trauma. Every last conceivable thing that was, in some way, connected to what had unfolded throughout the course of Ben's illness, gave rise to flashbacks, hypervigilance, numbness, headaches, nausea and memory loss. Trauma, I'd read, was not just an event in the past, or a memory. Rather, it was the imprint left by that experience on the mind, brain, and body. His death had snatched my sense of safety from its resting place. My nerve endings jammed up against my skin. I waited on high alert for something terrible to happen again, to receive another phone call that someone I loved had died. After a while came the exhaustion, unlike anything I'd ever felt before. It permeated every fibre of my being. This was survival mode, baby. I was barely hanging on by a thread. Sometimes it wasn't even day by day – it was minute by minute, moment by moment, breath by bloody breath.

I quickly began to recognise the triggers that would prompt an onset of either a) my PTSD symptoms or b) my grief. (At times the difference between the two was indiscernible. And honestly, what difference did the difference even make? It was all one great, big, messy clusterfuck.) The sound of ambulances was one of them. I'd hear a siren wailing in the village somewhere and before I knew it, I was hurtling down the motorway towards the Red Cross hospital in Tijuana, my knuckles white from squeezing the grab handle, my bare legs sticking to the leather seat. Any mention of hospitals, or the C-word, and I was standing outside the Macmillan Cancer Centre again, watching Ben, diaphanous, stumbling towards me in a state of chemo-induced delirium.

And of course, death. It was everywhere. Try as I might, it was impossible to escape it. As an executor to Ben's will, I had a mountain of admin that demanded my attention – bills to pay, subscriptions to cancel, accounts to close. With every task I ticked off the list, it was as if I were sweeping away his footprint, getting rid of all the evidence that he'd even existed in the first place. Meanwhile, death punctured every conversation, every newspaper article, every programme on TV. The word and all of its variations – dying, died, dead – made my stomach churn. 'Oh my God, I'm dying!' a friend wrote in a WhatsApp group in response to something funny. 'Did you hear that Emma's grandma died?!' 'Boo! I caught Covid,' said another friend. 'Me too,' replied someone else. *Thumbs-down emoji*.

The news reminded me of the stats countless times a day: another thousand dead, another hundred Covid-free. It turned up in every bright blue polypropylene mask and every bottle of hand sanitiser at the supermarket checkout, in every drawing of a rainbow in solidarity with the NHS stuck to the inside of a window in somebody's living room. I'd sit down to watch TV after dinner and BAM! A hospital scene within the first ten minutes. A murder. A body bag in the frame, bottom left. When you've seen a dead body, when you've stood over one and run your hands along cold, swollen skin mottled purple by pallor mortis, you can't just shrug it off like it's nothing. It's not just entertainment anymore, make-believe. It's real life – for you, at least. Every day, countless times a day, he died again. He died when I stood alone at the bathroom sink to brush my teeth, when I made one cup of coffee instead of two. He died when I reached for my phone to call him, only to remember that he couldn't answer anymore. He died when I heard a song he loved on Dougal's radio, when I opened the fridge to find his favourite brand of milk sitting on top of the shelf.

But it wasn't only death or even the thought of death that triggered me. It was all the life carrying on around me too. The nerve of it all! Ordinary people going about their ordinary days, problem free – or at least, that was what I told myself. I was, of course, the only person in the world to have any problems, to have ever felt this grief. Children were playing in the park behind Mum and Dougal's house, laughing. Husbands and wives were holding hands. Ugh. Couples – I couldn't bear to even look at them. How together, how saccharine, how smug they were. To tell you the truth – and it's an ugly truth – I was jealous of my friends. No matter how upset they felt for me, and for themselves for having lost a friend, they seemed able to put their grief down and return to their intact lives. For the ones who were in relationships, they could return to the arms of a partner who wasn't dead. They clinked champagne glasses and celebrated engagements, and cooed over newborn babies.

Why did it happen to us? I found myself asking over and over again. Why did it happen to me? There was nothing remotely fair about it. I tried to push the thoughts down, harboured them like a dirty secret. I didn't like myself much for feeling that way. It wasn't that I wanted something bad to happen to them – God, no. It was that I wanted what they had. I wanted someone to tell me, 'I know how you feel,' and to actually believe them. And people did tell me that, only they didn't have the faintest idea how I felt, because their partner hadn't died.

'Oh, I totally understand what you're going through,' people wrote beneath photos I shared on Instagram of me and Ben. 'I just divorced my husband.' Or, 'I know exactly how you feel because my grandpa just died. He was so young, he was only seventy years old. *Sad face*' Look, I get it – we want to show others that we can relate to them in some way. We think that by drawing a comparison between our experiences, we're acknowledging their pain and offering them our compassion. We want our own pain to be acknowledged in return. But the fact of the matter is that a break-up, no matter how messy or painful – and believe me, I'd had my fair share of those over the years – is not the same as a death. There isn't a world in which I'd rather Ben was dead than alive and no longer with me. I'd rather endure the pain of our separation than to know that his life had ended and to carry this grief. A relationship with a partner and a grandparent is fundamentally different. We don't have sex with our grandparents, for starters.

I suppose the point I'm trying to make is that comparing losses is useless. No two relationships are the same, therefore no two losses will be felt the same. American psychotherapist Megan Devine insists that whether or not we like to admit it, there *is* a hierarchy of grief. In her book *It's OK That You're Not OK*, she invites readers to imagine two injuries: stubbing a toe and having your foot ripped off. Both hurt, but the pain is different. The pain inflicted by the former is only temporary. You bounce back quickly. The latter, however, demands a lot of recovery time. It will affect every aspect of your life moving forward. Nobody would say that these two injuries are exactly the same, would they?

'At least you weren't married,' wrote others, as if Ben's death was easier to come to terms with because we hadn't managed to obtain a marriage certificate in time. We would've got married, only terminal cancer tends to get in the way of plans, doesn't it? Married or not, I thought, the weight of loss was much of a muchness. There is nobody who knows us as intimately as our partner. They are the voyager to the sacred corners of our body, the keeper of our deepest secrets. They see us at our best and at our worst. 'You're so young,' said another, 'you'll find love again!' – as if to say that Ben could be replaced, my pain patched up by somebody else.

Their attempts to comfort me by insisting that they could relate to my pain in some way only compounded my loneliness. I was desperate to connect with other people navigating partner loss, who felt what I was feeling. I thought that if I saw myself in the eyes of another, it might offer me the lifeline I needed. If they could survive such impossible grief, then maybe I could too.

One evening, while I was lying in bed wondering where on earth I'd find these people, I remembered a post I'd seen on Instagram over the summer. A friend of Ben's, a talent manager called Brett, had shared the news on social media that Alex Pullin, an Olympic snowboarder who went by the nickname Chumpy, had drowned while spearfishing on the Gold Coast in Queensland, Australia on 8th July. His partner Ellidy was a striking, blonde-haired woman from the Northern Beaches in Sydney. I turned on the lamp on the bedside table, reached for my phone, and searched for her profile on Instagram. They were eight years into their relationship when he'd died, and by the looks of things, more in love than ever, just like us. Ben and Chumpy even had similar features – hazel-green eyes, brown hair, and olive skin. A gentle temperament, a shared love of nature and music. I hovered over the 'Message' button on her profile for a moment, deliberating what to say to her. Would she find it comforting to know that she wasn't alone? That I understood – truly? I typed her a long, heartfelt message, signing off with, 'If it would ever feel good to connect and talk, then please let me know.'

I lay there in the dark for a little while longer, wondering if maybe, in the absence of a physical community, a community on social media could salve my loneliness. Curious, I typed in several hashtags into the search bar – #griefandloss, #lossrecovery – and scrolled, to discover that there were dozens and dozens of grief accounts. Beneath the photos, there were countless comments from people navigating all kinds of losses – people who had lost parents, siblings, children – and people, like me, who had lost their partners – many of whom were young, many of whom before they'd had a chance to get married. As I flicked through their stories, the ember of hope that had gone out the moment he had died began to catch fire again. There were others, in far-flung corners of the world, who understood this pain. There were others who were further out from their loss, who had managed to find meaning again – even love. What did Dostoevsky say – that to live without hope is to cease to live? Well, there was hope. I wasn't alone, after all.

A couple of days later, I logged on to Instagram to see a reply from Ellidy.

'It doesn't feel real,' she wrote. 'I'm not sure when it will. We will never get over it, but somehow we will learn to live with the grief. I'm here for you, girl. I promise you're not alone.'

She put me in touch with another woman, Georgie, who lived near to her in Brisbane. Georgie's partner Lachie had died just a few weeks after Ben. There were countless parallels between us both – in our relationships, our caregiving roles, in the way we viewed the world. The three of us began exchanging messages. Our messages quickly evolved to voice notes and video calls, and before long we were speaking every day, sometimes for hours on end. We shared our darkest thoughts with one another, how desperately we missed the boys. We swapped notes on partner loss and probate. We spoke late at night, when intrusive thoughts and painful memories were made all the more vivid and glaring.

'Good luck, sis,' Ellidy texted me on the morning of Ben's funeral on 15th December. 'I'm with you every step of the way.'

15

By the time I'd returned home from Mexico at the start of December, England's lockdown rules had been changing every few days. The government had just introduced a four-tier system across the country, with different restrictions in place depending on which county you lived in. Tiers 1 and 2 allowed you to meet up with people from different households outdoors, but only in groups of up to six people. Shops and leisure facilities were allowed to operate as normal. Pubs and bars could remain open so long as they were able to serve 'a substantial meal', and restaurants could open but were limited to table service only. Masks were mandatory at all times when moving about the restaurant, but *could* be taken off to drink or eat. Alcohol could only be served with said substantial meal, and venues had to be closed by 11 p.m. Four thousand people were allowed to gather outdoors and one thousand people indoors to attend sporting events. Weddings and funerals, on the other hand, were limited to thirty people.

I was used to the lockdown rules not making any sense, but this one was a step too far. I can only assume that we were somehow able to magically fly under Covid's radar when seated to eat, or when watching sports, or before 11 p.m. Unsurprisingly, we had an impossible time choosing the thirty attendees. There were hundreds of people that wanted to pay their respects to Ben. Luckily, we were told, the service could be streamed live online. 'Oh, great!' I told the funeral director on the phone through gritted teeth. How lucky indeed.

At a quarter to one, Ben's family and friends started trickling onto the patio outside one of the suites at Pembroke Lodge, a gorgeous Georgian mansion in Richmond Park, south-west London. We said hello to each other behind our masks at arm's length, attempting to make small talk as we waited on the steps outside.

'How are you?' Ben's friends asked, voices hushed.

'Yeah, I'm alright, thanks,' I replied. 'How are you?' The words sounded out of place, my voice unfamiliar. Of course I wasn't alright. I wasn't alright at all. Silence fell on the guests as the deep, resonating throb of an engine grew louder. I gasped as the hearse, a Harley-Davidson motorbike, came into view. There Ben was, making his entrance in a blaze of style as only he could. A motorbike trip from LA to Sacramento had been on his bucket list. *He should be on the bloody motorbike trip*, I kept thinking, watching in disbelief as the hearse crawled towards us.

'He'd love it, Lotts,' Mum whispered, her arm wrapped tightly around me.

We shuffled through the entrance to the suite, every face etched in pain and shock as the opening music began: an ambient remix of the iconic trance song 'Cafe Del Mar' by Energy 52, one of the most recognisable tracks in dance music, and one of Ben's favourites. I sat down on one of the chairs at the front next to Mum. Five rows of six chairs had been set out a metre apart – still close enough for her to reach over and squeeze my hand. Christiaan placed the urn on the table at the front in a wreath of flowers – peach, white, and orange with splashes of green, the same flowers I'd wanted at our wedding. Photos and video clips of Ben appeared on the screen above the table. I watched, again in disbelief, his smile twenty times its size beaming down at us. My heart was shattering all over again.

I pressed a wedge of tissues against my eyelids, trying to push back the tears springing forth. The celebrant, a tall and angular man with kind eyes and tousled brown hair called Jake, walked over to the stand as the song ended.

'Welcome on behalf of all of Ben's family to Pembroke Lodge,' he said. 'We meet today to remember, pay tribute, and to say goodbye to Benjamin Thomas Kouijzer.'

Hang on a minute, I thought to myself. *Goodbye? Why on earth would I want to say goodbye?* The word roused a flash of anger. *Why should I?* The only thing more tragic than Ben dying, was him dying and being left behind in 2020, only to eventually be forgotten about as time moved forward. He mattered to me when he was alive, and he mattered to me now.

I sat there listening to the tributes, as a hurricane of emotions tore through my body. I felt shocked, numb, devastated. But above all else, I noticed, I felt so incredibly lucky. Christ, I was the luckiest girl in the world. I'd always thought that a good life would be measured not by what we have, it would be measured by what we are. At the end of it, we will not be proud of how many cars we owned, or how much money we had in the bank. We will be proud of the ways we served others, of the ways we made a difference in the world. It was evident that Ben had lit up our lives like a shooting star. In a brief but beautiful lifetime, he had seen and done and given more than so many others ever would.

As the service came to an end, I thought of the Mughal Emperor Shah Jahan, who built the Taj Mahal in Agra, India, in memory of his late wife. The mausoleum is a tribute to her, a manifestation of their love forever immortalised in marble, or at least for as long as it remains standing. I would make sure, I decided, that in my own small way, Ben's afterglow continued burning; that our love would live on.

A few hours later, Mum, Dougal and I arrived home in Gloucestershire. As I climbed up the steps towards the cottage, I felt a wave of defeat wash over me. I pulled off my coat and boots, stumbled into the living room and collapsed onto the sofa. The funeral had given me a sense of purpose in recent weeks. People had said that a funeral brought closure, but the tear in my heart was still open and oozing. *What next?* I asked myself, as Dougal and I sat together, quietly digesting the day's events. We shouldn't have had to have a funeral to begin with, because he shouldn't have died. My thoughts were still fixated on all the what-ifs, the if-onlys, the maybes. I was stuck on a loop, like the needle of a record player hanging in a groove. If only he hadn't had surgery, if only he hadn't had chemo, if only we hadn't gone to Mexico. If only I'd done more, if only I'd tried harder, and so on and so forth. The guilt was maddening.

'Darling,' came Mum's voice from the kitchen. She walked into the living room holding a tray with three cups of tea and a plate full of snacks: savoury biscuits, different cheeses, olives, hummus and grapes. 'Give Ben's doctor at the cancer centre a call tomorrow, like we discussed.' She set the tray on the coffee table in front of the sofa and sat down next to me. 'I'm sure she'll be happy to talk to you and answer all your questions. It might give you a little bit of closure to get a grasp on what was actually going on, don't you think?'

I nodded and flopped my head onto her shoulder. Perhaps she was right. I'd spent so many months in denial, villainising the entire team of doctors responsible for his treatment. But they knew a great deal more about cancer than I did. Perhaps they had been telling the truth all along, after all.

The next day, I dialled the switchboard at the Macmillan centre and asked to speak to Dr Newman.

'I'm so sorry for your loss, Lotte,' she offered gently. 'I'll be totally frank with you. The scan he had in October showed a lot of progression of his disease. Covid along with the other infections certainly made his situation worse, but the reason he didn't get better or off the ventilator was because of how much cancer he had on board. The cancer drug felt so tantalising, but it is difficult to believe it could have enabled him to come off the ventilator and have any quality of life. My main concern was that he would end up ventilated for weeks and weeks, continuing to suffer until he eventually succumbed to the disease. It must have been really hard for you to go through this, but I think what you did for him was remarkable. You did absolutely everything you could to help him so please take that away with you – I hope it can offer you some comfort.'

I thanked her for her time and hung up the phone. All of a sudden, it struck me: I'd expected her to invest in his survival to the same extent as me, but she couldn't even if she'd wanted to. I could see that now. In the UK alone, hundreds of thousands of people were diagnosed with cancer every year, and over a hundred thousand of those cancer patients died. The pandemic had demanded even more of the NHS's already waning resources, with thousands of excess cancer deaths reported. She'd made it clear to me that his disease had outrun all of us, even the smartest doctors like her.

The pain of his death would always be there, I realised. That was a given. But my suffering? It was needless. There was a distinct difference between the two.

◆ ◆ ◆

A few days later, Mum drove me to her GP in Nailsworth so I could get hold of a prescription for some sleeping tablets. I'd tried almost everything we thought could help me: I'd steeped myself in bubble baths, doused my skin in aromatherapy oils. I'd drunk herbal teas, rubbed lavender all over my pillows. Mum gave me homoeopathic remedies, begged me to leave my phone out of my bedroom. But still, nothing worked. It took me hours to fall asleep, only to wake up soon after in a cold sweat from the same recurring nightmare: Ben dying all over again.

'I see,' the doctor replied flatly after I explained my situation to her. 'Perhaps you're in the fourth stage of grief. There are six stages in total – denial, anger, bargaining, depression, acceptance and meaning. From what you're telling me – that you're struggling to get out of bed every morning, that you can't function well or fall asleep – it sounds as though you might have depression. Have you thought about going on antidepressants at all?'

I looked at her, incredulous. What on earth was she talking about? Stages? *Of grief?* And depression? I couldn't believe what I was hearing.

'I haven't, no. I really don't think I'm depressed . . . I'm grieving.'

'Alright, well, if you're still feeling this way a few months from now, book in for another appointment and we can talk about giving you some medication. Some people experience prolonged grief disorder after losing a loved one.'

As I headed back outside towards Mum's car at the far end of the car park, I typed 'the stages of grief' into Google on my phone. In 1969, Swiss-American psychiatrist Elisabeth Kübler-Ross introduced the first five stages of grief in her book *On Death and Dying*. The sixth stage, meaning, was added four decades later by grief expert David Kessler. Although the model was originally intended to reflect the experiences of people who were dying, it became so deeply embedded in the collective consciousness as a way to describe the grieving process, that it is regularly referenced throughout pop culture, the media and bereavement support to this day.

'Pffft,' I snorted as I climbed into the passenger seat. *What a load of shit.* The very idea that grief followed a neat and linear trajectory was absurd to me. As far as I could see, grief was an entire smorgasbord of states and emotions that coiled together, overlapped, or recurred in unpredictable ways. One moment I thought I was fine, and the next I was crying into a bowl of Mum's homemade granola. Some days I felt like I was making progress, and others like I'd taken ten steps back. And from speaking to other grievers online, how it expressed itself seemed to differ from one person to the next. Some cried and some felt numb, some felt angry and some didn't. Some took time to begin processing their loss, some took longer to reintegrate back into day-to-day life. There were no rules, there was no right or wrong way to grieve, and there was certainly no timeline to it.

'Listen to this, Mum. It says here that prolonged grief is a mental health disorder diagnosed in people who present a persistent and pervasive grief response from six months after the death of a loved one. *Six months.*'

'Oh, for goodness' sake. That's ridiculous.'

'I know. The doctor even suggested I go on antidepressants. He's been gone a month, Mum. A month.'

While I realised my grief could give rise to mental illness, it was not a mental illness in itself. Nor was my grief a problem that could be fixed – because try as I might, I couldn't bring Ben back from the dead.

'He wouldn't want you to be sad,' a friend insisted over text later that afternoon.

Standing at the kitchen counter waiting for my camomile tea to steep, I stared at the words on my phone. Really? If the shoe was on the other foot, and it was me in a box on Ben's bedside table, I'd have been quite offended if he didn't feel even the least bit sad that I'd died. It would've seemed like the six and a bit years we had spent together had meant nothing to him. 'Of course I'm sad,' I wanted to say to said friend. His death was the saddest thing in the world to me. I had every right to be sad. Sadness was fucking NORMAL! It was a sign of my aliveness, of what it meant to be human.

'Everything happens for a reason,' wrote somebody else on Instagram. 'At least you got to say goodbye.'

'I didn't get to say goodbye,' I spat as I scrolled through their messages from the sofa. But even if I had, I knew without doubt that it wouldn't have made his death any easier to come to terms with. What would I have done exactly? I wanted to ask them. Wave him off as he gasped his final breaths? 'Bye, then! Safe trip!'

The thing is, I knew they meant well. They were trying to offer me some comfort, to help me recognise the lessons and silver linings in losing him. But those things meant diddly squat. A shit rolled in glitter is still a shit, no matter which way you look at it. The same applied to his death. This couldn't be dressed up, undone or made right.

'People don't understand unless they've been through it themselves, Lotts,' said Mum, after I read some of the messages to her over breakfast the following morning. 'Losing a loved one changes you. Irrevocably.' Of course, Mum knew, because she wasn't a stranger to grief. She knew it intimately. Her dad, my dear Grandpa Lou, had died suddenly years earlier. She'd cared for her mum for months, and had held her hand as she died on Valentine's Day in 2019.

I knew she was right. And I could hardly blame them – we live in a death-denying society for a start. We freeze our foreheads and slap face creams on, jumping on every last anti-ageing trend purported to make us look forever young. Even the healthcare professionals pathologise grief, impose arbitrary timeframes, condense the grieving process down into six stages with a beginning and an end. Grief, I realised, is a reminder of what is at stake. To love means to lose someday, and the truth of this is so unbearable that we'd rather look away. We'd rather pretend that we're invincible, that we belong to a special group exempt from ever experiencing such loss and grief.

I believed I belonged to that group too. I'd spent my life thinking that, so long as I was a good person, thought good thoughts and did good things, that good things would happen to me in return. That life would *reward* me, even. I'd prayed for Ben's healing every day for eight consecutive months. I'd journaled and meditated and prayed some more. 'What you think, you become,' the spiritual self-development books had said. A fat lot of good any of *that* did.

His death smacked me awake, tearing down everything I'd thought I was entitled to. I wasn't entitled to anything. The special group didn't exist. It's hard to accept that terrible things happen, that our plans don't always unfold as intended, and that life might not actually work out the way we want it to. We want to hold on to hope. But terrible things *did* happen, I thought, and for no reason. Expectant mothers died in labour. People starved. In some parts of the world, entire communities were wiped out by a single natural disaster. None of these things happened as part of God's work, or so the poor souls in question could ascend to the next stage of their spiritual journey. Life, I realised, would unfold however it unfolded. In-between the good times, there would be hard times – the kinds of times that would bring us to our knees, that threatened to tear us in two. And they could not be explained away, except for the fact that there was an innate randomness to life far beyond our control.

'Yeah,' I answered Mum after a while. 'I suppose dying in your thirties isn't really the done thing, is it? It's untimely. It doesn't follow the natural order of things.'

'Perhaps you ought to try to find somebody to speak to, love. Somebody who's trauma-informed – who works with people who have gone through loss.'

We opened our laptops and sat at the dining table for the next few hours researching. We read a dozen or so therapists' profiles, made some phone calls and swapped notes.

'What about this one?' I asked, turning my laptop towards her. The woman in question was a psychotherapist with a master's degree in something science related. She was a member of the British Association for Counselling and Psychotherapy, and specialised in trauma, post-traumatic stress disorder and grief. Mum gave me an encouraging nod. 'This is it!' I said. She sounded perfect.

I gave her a call and booked an introductory session for a few days' time. When the day arrived, after lunch I walked upstairs to my bedroom with my laptop, my head clear, thoughts gathered. Propping myself against my pillows, I opened the lid of my laptop and logged on to the call.

'Hello,' came a soporific voice. A mousy-haired woman was smiling at me through the screen. She seemed unsure, a little lily-livered. There was an awkward silence while I waited for her to prompt me. Wasn't that supposed to be what therapists did? 'So, Lotte – um – why don't we start with you telling me what happened again, and we can go from there?'

'Er, yeah. Okay. Well, like I said on the phone the other day, I lost my partner. Ben, his name was. He died a month ago on the fourteenth of November. He was diagnosed with soft tissue cancer in July 2019 . . . He had surgery and radiotherapy that summer, and we thought it was gone. We got engaged and started planning our wedding, but in March, two weeks into the first national lockdown, we found out that the disease had spread to his lungs. We were forced to isolate for the next seven months while he underwent treatment with the NHS. He had lung surgery and chemo, but neither of them worked. The disease continued to spread, so we flew to an alternative treatment centre in Mexico in September . . . The treatment was actually working there, but he caught Covid. He was admitted to intensive care and intubated.' I paused. She stared at me, not even a nod of encouragement. 'He was on the ventilator for twenty-four days. And then . . . then he died. He had pneumonia, sepsis, kidney failure . . . I saw him afterwards, and I keep thinking about it. The image of his body just lying there . . .' My voice trailed off. I glanced at her, waiting for her to say something.

'I see,' she replied flatly, her eyes glazed over, thoughts seemingly elsewhere. 'And how does that make you feel?'

'Um . . . I feel traumatised . . . devastated. Like I might die from the pain.' I clasped my hands together. My heart was racing. Why was I feeling so unsafe?

'I see,' she kept saying. She kept asking more questions, kept probing me. 'And how did that make you feel?' By the time I hung up the call forty minutes later, I was shaking. Therapy wasn't supposed to make me feel like this, I thought to myself.

'Oh, sweetheart,' Mum soothed as I crumpled onto the sofa next to her in tears. 'I'm so sorry it was so awful. How appalling! She clearly has no empathy. But let's not give up – there's got to be someone who can support you, perhaps someone with lived experience. Let's keep looking, shall we?'

I was helping Dougal clear away the dishes after dinner that evening, when the penny suddenly dropped. I'd connected with a woman called Marie on Instagram shortly after Ben had died. A grief coach from Montreal, she had lost her partner Andreas in 2017 following a brief but brutal struggle with pancreatic cancer. I was sure I'd read that she was taking on more one-to-one clients in the new year. I put away the last few pans before heading to her Instagram profile and typing out a message to send to her.

'I'm feeling so black and so overwhelmed by the prospect of navigating life without him,' I wrote. 'Every little part of him is still very much alive in my heart, mind and soul, and yet he's nowhere and will never be ever again. I can't make sense of any of it.'

An hour later, as I climbed into bed, I picked up my phone to see a message from her.

'Oh, Lotte, I'm so sorry,' she wrote. 'I can remember what grief felt like in the early days. I'm holding you in my heart.' She went on to explain the format of her sessions. 'The work is unique to the individual needs of the grieving human that's sitting before me. The journey is really about you and having someone in your corner while you navigate the most difficult time of your life. Everything is figured out as we go along, and as we discover, together, what serves you best in grief.'

That's exactly it, I thought, letting out an enormous sigh of relief. *She gets it.* The greatest value was not in receiving advice or in being cheered out of my grief, but in being seen, heard and validated. I needed someone to bear witness to my pain, to tell me, 'I'm sorry, this is shit, I'm here.'

16

Christmas the following week passed by unacknowledged. In years gone by, Mum and Dougal's house was full of laughter, singing, and Wham!'s 'Last Christmas' on repeat; delicious notes from Mum's mulled wine simmering on top of the hob, roast chicken and her legendary mince pies filling the air. This year couldn't have been more different, I thought, as I flopped onto the sofa in my dressing gown. We had talked about it briefly, and had decided that Christmas ought to be cancelled. Ben wouldn't get another Christmas ever again. To celebrate would have been an insult to his memory. The day came and went just like any other day, except for a few ornaments and fairy lights hanging from the small wooden tree that stood in the corner of their conservatory year round. I went to bed at nine o'clock on New Year's Eve a few days later, and woke up in 2021, crushed. It was the first year since Ben was born in which he didn't exist anymore. *How on earth am I supposed to reconcile with that?* I thought as I dragged myself out of bed that morning. It was an altogether head-fuck. For the normal, non-grieving folk, a new year usually brings about a renewed sense of hope and determination. Eager to grab the next twelve months by the balls, they go about setting goals and resolutions – run a marathon, get a promotion at work, quit smoking – that sort of thing. But for me, it brought with it a fresh layer of pain.

I lay on the bathroom floor a couple of days into January, sobbing great, ghastly balls of grief. They rose from my throat and into my mouth, along with glue-like remnants of the porridge Dougal had made me for breakfast that morning. The two of them had left the house to go food shopping and wouldn't be home for another hour, which only meant one thing: unleashing the full force of my grief. I knew it hurt them both to see me in so much pain. I knew they were grieving for Ben too – he was as good as their son-in-law for six years, and they'd come to love him as a part of our family.

I wiped the snot from my chin and steadied myself against the toilet lid. This, I thought as I pushed myself up to my feet, was my very own version of rock bottom. *How glamorous.* I turned around and caught sight of my reflection in the mirror. 'Christ,' I gasped. I barely recognised the woman staring back at me. I looked translucent and brittle, like a sheet of frosted glass. I climbed out of my pyjamas and into the shower, turned on the taps and slumped against the wall.

My grief had felt safe in 2020, I realised. There, it was close to Ben. But time would keep dragging me forwards, no matter how much I kicked and screamed and dug in my heels in protest. It wasn't right nor fair that he had died, and it would never be. But facts were facts: he *had*, and there was nothing that could be done to bring him back. Hadn't I suffered enough? For two years and counting, life had felt so small and insufferable, a clockwork of cancer and caregiving and grief. Perhaps the drawn-out nature of it all helped me to reach this realisation quickly: that I wanted this feeling to change.

Other grievers I'd spoken to on social media had assured me that it wouldn't get any easier, and I sort of understood why they'd said it. In some way, it acknowledged the enormity of what I'd lost. Grief and grievers alike deserve to be acknowledged, and what I'd lost was, unquestionably, enormous. But the thought of carrying this pain and longing for a lifetime wasn't the least bit comforting. It was terrifying. I didn't want to fall prey to that narrative. While I couldn't control what had happened to Ben, I *could* control what *I* did from here on out. Empowerment is found in the choices we get to make. As far as I could see, I had two: I could stay at rock bottom, drowning in my victimhood on the bathroom floor or under the showerhead. I could attempt to anaesthetise myself by any means necessary – denial, delusions of magical thinking, food and online shopping – and I could continue to tell myself that life would never be good again without him, thus fulfilling my own prophecy. *Or* . . . I could begin, one breath at a time, to claw my way out. It would undoubtedly take time. It would take work – much of which I imagined to be far uglier than the heavily curated squares on my Instagram feed suggested it would be. I loved a scented candle and a bubble bath as much as the next person, but those things wouldn't cut it on their own.

'It can't get any worse than this,' I said out loud as I stepped out of the shower and reached for my towel hanging on the corner of the radiator. It was as much of a promise to myself as it was an observation. The only way forward from rock bottom, I decided, was up.

A few days later, I logged on to my first call with Marie. She started by asking me questions about how Ben and I had met, about our relationship and our life together. She wanted to know what Ben was like as a person. I smiled as I told her about the dating app, about the moment we became boyfriend and girlfriend on a dance floor in Amsterdam one autumn. I told her how he loved to be silly. How he'd often make his entrance into the living room or bedroom arse backwards – sometimes clothed and sometimes not – twerking.

I told her that he didn't need to wear the mala beads, do the yoga or chant the mantras, because he *was* it: pure light. A bona fide angel in human form. There was no mention of cancer or death, nothing of the sort. Not yet, she said. We'd get to that later. She spoke softly, but not in a patronising way – in a way that communicated her proximity to my pain. She understood it because she'd felt it first-hand. I could feel bits of tension lodged somewhere deep in my body beginning to unstick, melt away. She told me she was in my corner, and that she felt honoured to support my journey.

'Lotte, your only goal right now is just to take care of yourself moment to moment.' We arranged to speak every week at the same time for the foreseeable, and hung up the call.

I floated through the next few weeks feeling untethered. I needed something to hold on to, to plant my feet on. I needed structure. *Sod everyone else and their resolutions*, I thought. Now was not the time for bloody resolutions. I could barely think about the next week, let alone the next twelve months. I decided to come up with my own definition of success instead.

On a cold Saturday afternoon at the end of January, Mum, Dougal and I pulled on our coats, gloves and scarves, and clambered into the car. An inexplicable urge to read and write had been steadily swelling inside of me lately. I found myself drawn to stories of resilience, to others who, like me, had gone through hard times. On Instagram, I shared some of my deepest, darkest thoughts and feelings with anybody who cared to read them. It wasn't only an act of personal catharsis, I realised. It was a bridge too – connecting me to others who had walked similar paths. Our experiences, though unique, shared commonalities of trauma, grief – longing for what was, for all that could have been. I didn't consider myself a writer by any means – but I wanted to write about my experiences like others had. Actually, more than that – I *had* to write. It had started to become somewhat of a compulsion, but the good kind. 'Don't bottle up your heartbreak,' my inner voice kept telling me. If I did, I feared it might only metastasise into something deeper and more pervasive. My body was not a burial ground for my pain. I had to pour it into something, let it metamorphose. Let it live in words.

We parked the car next to the church in Cirencester and hurried out of the cold into Waterstones bookshop, the warmth enveloping us like a hug. I loved it in here, we all did. I cast my eyes around the shop. I could spend hours getting lost in books, each containing entire worlds waiting to be discovered, characters I'd grow to love. The smell of paper mingled with freshly brewed coffee from the cafe upstairs. The three of us agreed to meet at the entrance in half an hour and parted ways – Mum and I in non-fiction, her down one end and me down the other, and Dougal in the history section in the far corner.

I ran my fingertips along the shelves in search of a couple of books: Nora McInerny's *No Happy Endings* and Laura Lynne Jackson's *The Light Between Us*. I'd discovered the authors on Instagram during one of the many sleepless nights spent scrolling through hashtags, looking for comfort. I'd gone right back to the very beginning of Nora's page, devouring each of the captions underneath her photos. Her husband Aaron died of brain cancer in 2014 when she was thirty-one, just weeks after a miscarriage and the death of her dad. Not long after, she set up a foundation, wrote a book, and started giving talks about all things loss and grief. Within a year, she met her now husband, Matt. All of her thoughts and feelings seemed to mirror my own, so much so that it was as if she was speaking directly to me. *About* me, even. I appreciated the way she refused to skirt around the hard bits – the bits that were often hidden behind closed doors. She bared all of it – the survivor's guilt, other people's harmful expectations of her. Her longing to be desired by another man. She was so candid, so matter of fact about it all, as if grief and all that came with it was the most normal thing in the world. *And it is*, I thought to myself as I stood there, leafing through the first few pages. Grief is entirely normal, because death is entirely normal.

Laura Lynne Jackson is a famous psychic medium who has given readings to thousands of people, connecting them with loved ones who have crossed to what she refers to as the Other Side. I found her book tucked away on the bottom shelf in the far corner and opened it to a passage about love.

In it, she wrote that the love we have for one another in this lifetime still exists on the Other Side. Our grief is not the cessation or the absence of that love, rather it is the continuation of it. It doesn't just end – it goes on.

I smiled to myself as I flicked through the book. I'd heard about the concept of continuing bonds somewhere in a blog post. It rejected old bereavement models that promoted the idea that grievers had to let go of their deceased loved ones in order to move forwards. Instead, it encouraged grievers to redefine their relationships, to actually carry their loved ones with them. I didn't have to get rid of Ben in order to be considered well-adjusted in my grief. If continuing our bond meant that the pain of his death felt a little less unbearable, then I ought to do just that.

The three of us wandered back outside a little while later into the crisp air, laden with half a dozen books and a couple of notepads, in search of a bite to eat.

After washing up the last few plates from dinner that evening, I sat back down at the dining table, notebook and pen in hand. I closed my eyes and took a deep breath, before letting streams of consciousness tumble out of me: all of my emotions, impressions, fears and doubts. Even the glimmers of joy, like the taste of the coffee and walnut cake I'd had at the cafe earlier on Castle Street with Dougal and Mum. I poured it all onto the pages, uncensored. It's not that writing it down necessarily made things better, but it made things different somehow – as if pieces of my pain were beginning to uproot from my body and find a home someplace else. And that was surely a good thing, I thought to myself.

And what if, I wrote, it wasn't so much about merely tolerating my grief – overcoming it, even – but rather, honouring it? Granting it all the time it needed to metabolise? What if instead of seeing grief as an inconvenience, we could see it as part and parcel of our humanness, something that accompanied us through life? Something that, if given the right care and time, could help us all to live more meaningful, purposeful, and enriched lives?

Before long, I was beginning to make a note of all the ways I showed up for myself. The days were scratched off with a checklist of small victories. Did I manage to get out of bed? Tick. Did I have a shower and get dressed? Tick, tick. Did I drink enough water? Great. Did I go for a walk? Even better. From the outside, it didn't look like much, but the seemingly insignificant things in the wake of trauma and loss, I realised, added up.

Mum and Dougal were both keen walkers, but especially Dougal. Throughout his career in the Counter Terrorism Command at New Scotland Yard, he'd travelled the world from top to bottom, and his appetite for adventure had never left him, even after retirement. Most mornings, he'd set out with a map, a flask and some snacks packed in a rucksack and stride across the hills for hours. Walking was a form of therapy for him, he said. He'd return again in the afternoon, recounting tales he'd learned from people he'd met along the way. That was Dougal for you – ever inquisitive, ever the enthusiast, always making friends wherever he went. Thanks to their gentle yet persistent encouragement, I occasionally pulled on my boots, threw on my coat and joined them. I couldn't have cared less about my health. I'd lost all confidence in my body to assimilate nutrients, to function as it was supposed to. What was the point in caring, I'd concluded, when I'd witnessed an otherwise healthy man wither away like a raisin in front of my very eyes? I'd have liked to have unbuttoned myself, stepped *out* of my body if I could – but since that wasn't possible, the only other option was to move it.

One morning in early February, we woke to a blanket of snow five inches deep surrounding the house. My sister Georgia and her son River lived up the road from ours on the other side of the park. After a bowl of porridge each, the three of us threw on some layers and headed to meet them by the swings for a snowball fight. The sound of my laughter alarmed me at first. It rang off the moment I realised that it was coming from my own mouth. But the more snowballs I managed to land on the back of Dougal's head as he bent down to scoop up the snow, unsuspecting, the louder it grew: deep belly eruptions of unfettered joy. River shrieked with delight. By the time I stepped inside the front door and pulled my boots off hours later, my cheeks flushed with cold air, I was bolstered by the sense that I'd achieved something.

But all of the reading and talking and writing and walking, I realised, the countless hours spent facing and feeling it all – it wasn't enough. A kind of nagging agony still gnawed away at me. *Where is he?* I had tried to convince myself that one of these days, he'd walk through the front door and kick his shoes off, pull up a chair and sit down for dinner just like he always had. Maybe it would happen if I wished for it hard enough – but then again, no amount of wishing had stopped him from dying.

If he's really dead then, I thought to myself as I lay in bed wide awake one night, *I need to make contact with him somehow. I need to know that he's okay.*

I spent hours trying to visualise him, just as I had done with our future child when he was ill all those months before. I'd hoped that his ghost would appear, a shimmering apparition at the foot of my bed. I talked to him in my head, talked to him out loud – only the silence was deafening. There were moments that I was sure I could feel him nearby, the whoosh of his body brushing past me. He was there but just out of reach and out of sight, as though he'd fallen through a trapdoor.

'God, it's so disheartening when you get a shit one, but he's with you, babe, I promise,' said Ellidy one afternoon. I'd just got off the phone with a middle-aged woman called Susan from Yorkshire, who'd claimed to be able to communicate with dead loved ones. She'd pretended to make contact with somebody, shouting every letter of the alphabet besides B at me in strange voices.

'There's a really strong "Liz" presence coming through,' she'd insisted. 'Keep an open mind – it'll start to make sense later.'

No, Susan. It won't, I thought, before ending the call and blocking her number. I had lots of nicknames for Ben, and although I'd always thought he'd make a beautiful woman should he ever feel inclined to cross-dress, Liz definitely wasn't one of them.

Ellidy forwarded me the contact details of a psychic medium called Rebecca from Sydney. She'd had a session with her a few weeks before, and Chumpy had come through for her straight away. I booked the session for the following week under a different email address so she couldn't run my name through Google and find our story.

On the evening of the call, I paced around my bedroom in anticipation. Clouds of incense hung below the ceiling. The urn containing his ashes stood on top of the chest of drawers surrounded by tealight candles. *What if he actually comes through?* I asked myself. Would he be okay? What had it felt like to die? Where was he? Questions, questions, questions. I had thousands of questions. At five to eight, I sat down, opened my laptop, and logged on to Zoom.

'Hi!' A wide smile framed by short blonde hair and feather earrings suddenly appeared on the screen.

'Hello,' I replied eagerly. We introduced ourselves and exchanged some small talk, but I kept my cards close to my chest, determined not to give any clues away. I wanted her to give me hard evidence – names, details, places. Facts. Vague reassurances of a loved one's presence on the Other Side wouldn't be enough to persuade me that it was real. 'I've got your man here,' she said after a few minutes. 'He's been waiting to speak to you all day.' She paused and glanced sideways for a moment, as if she was listening to someone whispering something in her ear. 'I'm hearing a B or a D. It's Ben, right?'

Holy shit, I thought.

'Yes.'

She described his features – green eyes, brown curly hair in a top knot, and tanned skin. All smiles and teeth – it was really him. But his hair? He'd lost all of it due to chemo.

'Oh no,' she chuckled, shaking her head. 'You get to choose which version you are over there.'

So what about the cancer? I asked. He wasn't sick anymore?

'That's right,' she continued. 'You don't take any of the bad bits with you. You don't even really have a clear memory of it, actually – it's like waking up from a bad dream.'

For the next two and a half hours, I could barely get a word in edgeways. She talked and talked, disclosing intimate details about his life and our relationship. His mum and dad were called Jean and Clem, his brother, Christiaan. He grew up on the south coast of Spain. He worked as an agent in the music industry and loved martial arts.

'He's very good at communicating with you through nature, but you keep doubting the signs. He's asking you to stop that. The two of you had a deep connection when he was earthside, and that hasn't just disappeared now he's transitioned. If anything, your connection is actually stronger now that it travels between realms.' She went on to talk about his illness. 'You went overseas for treatment. It was a rare cancer, right? He's pointing to his chest . . . But it wasn't cancer that he died from, he's telling me. No. It was a build-up of toxins in the body. S . . . Ah! Sepsis.'

I nodded. 'Yes, that's right.'

'He wants you to know that he wasn't in any pain, because he was asleep for the last month of his life.' She told me things we hadn't shared with anyone else – things that had happened at the treatment centre in Tijuana, conversations we'd had with his medical team.

'He wants you to know that he's okay,' she reassured me. 'And you will see each other again one day, but it's not your time to join him right now. You've got a lot still to do until then. And you must know he would never have left you alone without a back-up plan, right? He's bringing somebody to you. God . . .' She paused. 'I've never had a spirit tell me this before. Bear with me for a second. I want to make sure I'm communicating this to you properly . . . He's telling me . . . He's telling me that he's bringing his soul brother to you. The three of you – wow . . . this is so beautiful – sorry, I don't usually get emotional in readings. He's showing me that the three of you have experienced many lifetimes together before.'

My mouth fell open.

'And remember – you can ask him for a sign, Lotte. He's always listening to you.'

I sat there for a while after we hung up the call, stunned. The word 'death' had suddenly taken on a different meaning. Before, I'd recoiled every time it had been uttered. It had felt so violent, so final to me. But why did it need to feel that way? It was only violent and final because that was the story I told myself. The phrase 'passed away' was too ambiguous, too abstract. It undermined the gravity of what had happened, and distanced me emotionally and mentally from what I'd lost. The fact was he *had* died – and it needn't be this big, scary thing that I tiptoed around anymore. Wasn't all the tiptoeing part of what made grief the elephant in the room that bumped up against people, prompting awkward responses laden with platitudes? I could choose a different story if I wanted to, one that owned and embraced the facts.

I blew out the candles, stubbed out the incense stick and wandered into the bathroom. I turned on the taps and sat on the edge of the bath, swilling the water around with my hands. A thought was gathering in my mind as I poured in some arnica bath oil. Elsewhere, death was embraced as an intrinsic part of life. It was celebrated, even. Every year at the beginning of November, people all over Latin America celebrated the Day of the Dead holiday, or *Día de los Muertos*. It's a family reunion, except dead ancestors are the guests of honour. People believe that, over the course of the week, their loved ones' souls return to the world of the living. They dress in elaborate outfits and paint their faces, or wear masks that look like skulls. *Ofrendas* or altars are set up at home to welcome their loved ones back. They decorate the altars with photos, candles and food. They pile into cemeteries and spend the night there, eating, drinking, playing games, listening to music and remembering their loved ones. Death and expressions of grief aren't kept out of sight and out of mind, they're out in the open for all to see. How beautiful. How freeing.

I took off my clothes and slid into the bath. Rebecca had made it clear to me: there *was* more. Life after death wasn't a far-fetched fantasy reserved for fiction books. Ben's essence, his soul – the thing that had once animated all of that five-foot-ten, sparkly-eyed, curly-haired loveliness – was still here. The more I thought about it, the more it made sense. After all, light and sound waves bounce around all over the place. Even though we can't see or feel them, we know they're there. Was it really so implausible that Ben was still here too? I closed my eyes and pictured him sitting opposite me, his back against the other end of the bathtub, his unruly ringlets sitting on top of his shoulders. Everything in the known universe was energy, and energy couldn't be created or destroyed – Einstein's first law of thermodynamics – it could only be transformed.

◆ ◆ ◆

One morning not long after the reading, I pulled on my coat and scarf and headed outside. My extremities braced against the late February chill clawing at my skin. Careful not to slip on the stone slabs wet with frost, I inched my way down the steps, turned left outside the cottage gate, and walked up the road towards my sister Georgia's house. Mist hung over the allotment behind the park. Jutting out from the soil, leafless stalks of last season's crops sparkled with frost. I walked up her driveway and followed the winding footpath past a row of cottages towards her front door. River's face was pressed against the glass.

'Where's Uncle Benny, Lotte?' he asked as he opened the door to greet me.

I glanced at Georgia, who was standing behind him.

'Uncle Benny's in the stars, darling, remember?' she said as she crouched next to him, pulling on his hat and gloves. 'It's where we come from, and it's where we go back to after our life. There are pieces of him in our hearts too,' she continued, pressing her hand against his tiny chest. 'We carry him with us, Rivvi – always.'

A lump formed in my throat. I knew she'd know what to say, she always did. Over the last couple of months, not a single day had passed without her messaging or calling me. Like Mum, she was my rock, her presence a safe haven I could retreat to any time I needed. She'd drop everything to be there for me, regardless of what she was doing. And there was, I thought, an element of truth in what she'd said. Every atom of oxygen in Ben's lungs, of iron in his blood, every atom of carbon in his muscles and of calcium in his bones had been forged in the hearts of long-dead stars. He was made of cosmic dust, created by supernovas.

River's eyes widened in awe. 'Maybe we'll see him tonight, then, Mummy?' he said, pushing wisps of golden hair from his face.

'Maybe, my love,' I replied.

Georgia handed me a flask of hot chocolate and we headed back down the pathway towards the park. She looped her arm through mine as River ran ahead of us, occasionally stooping to examine another tiny insect or plant that had captured his curiosity.

'It's so tragic, sweetheart,' she said, her voice tender. 'I'm so sorry that he's not here, and that you're having to endure all this loss and pain. But he is with you – not in his physical body of course, in a different way . . . he is here.'

'I know,' I answered quietly. We sat down on the bench beside the playground, watching as River clambered up the climbing frame and flew down the slide. It was not that his laughter felt healing. Nothing did. But it made me feel something other than pain. Perhaps, I thought, it was a reminder of all that was still good in the world.

'I like to think that he's in the wind, you know,' she continued as we snuggled against each other. 'In the trees and flowers, in the clouds. In all the little synchronicities you're experiencing.'

I liked to think so too. I smiled at her and squeezed her hand.

Later that evening, I stood on the patio at the front of the cottage with Dougal, a wool blanket wrapped tightly around me. Pulling on a pair of thick gardening gloves blackened by heat, he set about arranging a stack of logs inside the fire pit, the thicker logs at the bottom, and the thinner ones on top. He carefully placed the kindling on top of the pile, before setting it alight with a match. We sank into our chairs in front of the pit and watched as the rest of the logs slowly caught fire.

Fire, came a thought from nowhere. Cremation. Ben's body . . . *Burning.*

I shook my head. *No. I don't want those thoughts, not now. You're not welcome here.*

Dougal glanced at me and I smiled at him. I'd grown accustomed to pretending like I was doing better. And that was the thing about grief, I'd come to learn – about any mental anguish, in fact. It was an affliction invisible to the outside world.

I sighed as wisps of smoke flew upwards, the scent of sweet resin drifting in the air. Another trigger, another impossible thought staved off.

The two of us chatted quietly, Dougal's soothing Scottish lilt punctuated by the fire fizzing and popping. His voice, the fire, were welcome distractions from all the mental noise. I leaned my head against the back of the chair and looked up. A dozen or so stars scintillated like diamonds against the inky spill of night. Georgia was right, I thought as I counted them.

Six, seven . . . twelve, thirteen. His energy had transmuted, no longer bound by flesh and bone and time and space. He was everywhere now, all at once.

17

The cadence of my grief, I'd noticed, would come in waves. I would cry out for Mum who was pottering in the next room and will myself to hold on until she got to me. The waves would come rushing in, throwing me against the rocks like a rag doll. 'Breathe,' I'd whisper as they dragged me under and churned me over and over again. I'd wrap my arms around myself, as though my own body was a life raft. 'Just breathe. In and out.' Mum would sit at the side of the bed, cradling me like a baby until the waves had retreated.

To my surprise, they'd been growing further apart lately. It was a Sunday afternoon in early March, and Mum, Dougal and I headed down the hill towards Chalford, a picture-perfect chocolate-box village that straddled the Thames and Severn Canal. The sun was up, the sky totally clear. The arrival of the first signs of spring, I noticed, seemed to signal the start of something new. A rebirth of sorts. It hadn't come to me in a big epiphany. There was no dramatic 'aha' moment of any kind. It was simply a quiet realisation one day, a whispering from somewhere inside that went something along the lines of 'Life is really rather magical.'

I found myself drawn to music again, yearning for the sort of dopamine hit that only the discovery of a great song I hadn't heard before could give me. Something that Ben and I had connected over, that had brought us so much happiness over the years, had felt impossible in his absence. But to my surprise, I'd found comfort in the bass lines and chord progressions of our favourite songs. I'd reactivated my Spotify account, and had begun sifting through playlists on the online music store, Beatport. I'd noticed myself beginning to relish the small things, seemingly insignificant things that, in the early aftermath of his death, I hadn't cared to take any notice of. What if, I wondered, in spite of my grief – because of it, even – I could allow myself to experience one beautiful thing a day, no matter how trivial it might feel? To allow myself to savour it, without all of the guilt? A brilliant sunset. River's laugh. A great book. I knew that none of these things would make up for or cancel out my grief, but perhaps they could sit alongside it as companions. They could coax me, gently, out of the crack between the floorboards and back to the land of the living.

By now, walking had become a bit of a ritual. It was a fixed mark in my day that gave me a reason to get up and out of the house. The walks had been short to begin with. To the end of the road and back was about all I could manage. Then up to the park, round the village, sometimes even to Oakridge or Eastcombe. There was something about the wide-open spaces, the dense forests and undulating hills. Something about the quietude of it, all except for the sound of nearby birds, leaves dancing in the wind, and my own two feet carrying me forward. 'Put one foot in front of the other, Lotte,' I told myself, just as I had done when I walked out of the intensive care unit that day, after I'd kissed Ben's body goodbye. Baby steps. I knew that with time and perseverance, eventually those steps would grow bigger, becoming strides and leaps until I reached the peak and looked back to take in the view, in awe of how far I'd come.

That day, the three of us followed the footpath that ran along the edge of the canal and into the woods. The frost that had covered the woodland floor throughout the winter months had thawed. We ambled between the trees, their arms twisting towards the cerulean sky. Intricate shadows danced across the blankets of wild garlic and snowdrop shoots. It made me think of the words I'd come across earlier that morning on Instagram. Madeleine L'Engle, author of *A Swiftly Tilting Planet*, wrote that light and darkness danced together. Just like the light and the darkness, I realised, my grief and joy could coexist. I could honour his death and I could move forwards. I could miss the life I had with him and I could, gradually, begin to fall in love with my new one. It was not this or that; a choice of one thing or another.

'You're still here, darling,' Mum added, linking her arm through mine. 'Your life has to count for something. You've got to seize it with both hands and live it. Do it for Ben. It's up to you to carry his torch for him now.'

25th March, a few weeks later, marked Ben's first birthday since he had died. I found myself paralysed by indecision. How was I supposed to celebrate a day so inherently joyful when he wasn't here to celebrate it? Sensing my overwhelm, Georgia took the decision out of my hands and offered to drive us to Glastonbury. The festival site was at Worthy Farm in Pilton village, Somerset. Her car pulled up outside Mum and Dougal's cottage after breakfast, and I grabbed the urn sitting on top of the console table in the hallway and headed outside.

'Hi, darling,' she said as I pulled open the door. A small bouquet of pink and orange roses wrapped in brown paper was lying on the passenger seat. 'Here you go,' she offered, handing me a takeaway coffee.

'Oh, sis, you're so thoughtful. Thank you. And these flowers!' I picked up the bouquet as I climbed in, and buried my nose in their petals. 'They're gorgeous!'

'I knew you'd like them,' she smiled.

I cradled the urn in my lap as we set off down the lane towards the M5. Ninety or so minutes later, we pulled into Pilton and followed the directions on my phone towards Worthy Farm.

'I think it's this way,' I said to Georgia, as we rattled over the potholes along Cockmill Lane.

Kings Meadow soon came into view. The meadow was one of the highest spots of the festival, and, consequently, one of the best places to see the site in all its glory. Ben and I had spent countless nights there over the years, watching the sun come up, huddled beside a fire. We trundled down the dirt track when, suddenly, the stone circle – a megalithic monument constructed as a place of ritual and ceremony during the festival – appeared through the trees. 'That's it!' I pointed.

We parked the car and climbed through the brambles to get to the path on the other side of the hedge that ran along the edge of the meadow, urn in hand. The scaffolding of the legendary Pyramid Stage stood out against the patchwork of green in the distance. I set the urn down in front of the stones that stood in the middle of the circle and lit a handful of tealight candles. Georgia laid half a dozen of the roses around the urn. My eyes felt hot with tears.

'Happy birthday, my love,' I whispered, the words trailing off like the pappus of a dandelion scattering in the wind. I was desperate to hold him, to feel him, to bury my head in his curls. Instead, I rested my hand on top of the urn. It was the closest I could get to him now. Georgia and I sat together for a while, the silence between us broken by the humming of bees and occasional whirring of nearby tractors. We'd shared countless moments like this, just sitting together in silence. She didn't have to utter any words for me to feel comforted by her. Her presence alone was enough.

I thought about what Mum and Dougal had said. They were right. I *was* still here, and my life *did* count for something. What a disservice it would be to Ben to see it any differently. I didn't want to merely survive anymore. *Fuck it,* I thought to myself. If I couldn't do life with him, then I'd do it for him instead. I wanted to live, and urgently. It was my duty – my right, even – to hold on to the glimmers of joy with both hands, no matter how faint and fleeting they were. It was not merely a way to survive my grief, and to honour him – but a way to love myself the way that he had loved me when he was here. Didn't I deserve that love? And to make the most of what was left of my life until I joined him? *Fuck it*. Aha! There it was – my new motto for the rest of 2021. My inner GPS, if you will. I would move in the direction of all the things that felt good and positive, without overthinking it.

A few days after Ben's birthday, Mum, Dougal and I drove to London for my brother Oliver's wedding, organised in adherence with the latest Covid-19 regulations. I was apprehensive about it. How would it make me feel to watch another couple tie the knot so soon after losing him?

We met Georgia, River and Dad in the car park outside the venue near Dalston and headed in together to find Oliver standing at the altar, dressed in a navy three-piece suit with a burgundy tie and boutonnière. My worries evaporated the moment he wrapped me in a bear hug. This wasn't about me, I realised. It was about my brother. I loved him dearly, and his happiness was mine. He couldn't wipe the smile off his face, dimples forming in both of his cheeks when his fiancée Jen appeared at the back of the room in a long-sleeved lace gown.

After the ceremony, we said our goodbyes, and Mum and Dougal drove me to Finsbury Park. My period of convalescence, cocooned in their Cotswolds cottage, was over. It was time to face the music and return home. My breath tangled in my lungs as I stepped over the threshold of our flat. There was no welcome home banner, no twinkling lights. Only deafening silence and the smell of loss lingering in the air.

I threw my keys into the bowl on the console table by the front door and wandered from room to room. First the spare bedroom, just off to the right. A disco ball and decks stood on the chest of drawers by the window catching dust. Ben's creative space; our future baby's bedroom. Then down the hallway and into ours, his pyjamas neatly folded on top of his pillow. I passed the bathroom. An abandoned bamboo toothbrush. I walked into the kitchen and opened the fridge to find his favourite sriracha sauce gathering mould. *Another plaster ripped off*, I thought. I felt the overwhelming urge to sit all of a sudden. I knelt down next to the chest in the living room, examining the makeshift altar I'd spent countless sleepless nights praying in front of on my hands and knees. I noticed a piece of paper tucked under his statue of Ganesha. I picked it up and unfolded it. 'Every adversity, every failure, every heartbreak, carries with it the seed of an equal or greater benefit.' The words were written in his handwriting, the letters spidery and thin.

I studied it for a while, tracing my fingertips over the ink. He'd always been a glass-half-full sort of person. Even in the face of his terminal diagnosis, he'd remained positive. He'd endured so much pain and fear and grief, and had handled it with so much grace. In fact, he'd spent most of his illness thinking about *other* people, and how he could help *them*. He'd arranged for one of his artists to film a video for the nurse that was looking after him at the Royal

Brompton after lung surgery, because she'd told him she was a fan of his. He'd swapped numbers with an elderly man at the Macmillan Cancer Centre so they could keep in touch, after learning that he didn't have a family to go home to once he was discharged. He'd spent countless hours on his phone or at his laptop, sending words of support and encouragement to other cancer patients.

What a man. I wondered what he'd make of all this, of him dying – whether he felt that anything good would ever come from it. I slipped the piece of paper back under the statue where I found it. *What next?* I thought, as I looked around the room. A white cardboard box jutted out from under the sofa. I pulled it out and opened the lid, when my mouth fell open. 'Christ!' Inside were eight plaits of thick, shiny human hair – the same hair I'd cut from his head all those months ago before chemo. I picked up one of the plaits and ran it across my hands and cheeks. Yes. There he was – just. It was the closest I'd got to a little piece of him in almost a year. With the plait in my hands still, I pulled myself up onto the sofa and slumped against the cushions. I was home, at long last. It was familiar and alien, comforting and painful all in the same instant. All around me were precious pieces of evidence that he had lived, that the life I'd lost with him *had* existed. There was no use in throwing any of it out, I reasoned. No – because we'd only have to buy it all again. I knew he'd died. The rational part of my brain could accept this as fact. But there was another, smaller part of me that was still holding out for the day that he would knock on our front door and say, 'Hey, baby, I'm home.'

As daylight receded, I lay in a hot bath until the skin on my fingers wrinkled. I slipped into his pyjamas and into bed, wedged between two pillows like I always did for comfort. I fell asleep quickly and deeply, and woke to a quiet birdsong coming from my neighbour's garden below my window the next morning. I got dressed, made myself a cup of tea, and headed to the post office nearby with the box of hair. I addressed the box to the Little Princess Trust, the charity that provided wigs free of charge to children and young people who'd lost their hair due to cancer. My heart burst as I handed the package to the man behind the till. It felt so good to fulfil Ben's wish, to know that he was helping people like he always had, even in the wake of his death. His death would not be for nothing, I thought to myself, as I wandered the aisles of our local supermarket in search of something to cook for breakfast. This pain would not be in vain. If I could help people – people who were navigating trauma or loss and grief – then perhaps my life could feel purposeful again. Like the widow and author Nora McInerny, and other grievers whose books I'd pored over, maybe someday I could write about this experience too.

18

A couple of months later at the start of May, the UK's lockdowns and restrictions started to lift. They'd helped in some ways. I'd grown accustomed to the world feeling smaller over the last eight months of Ben's life, and in the wake of his death, I'd needed it to stay that way. My life had come grinding to a standstill and the rest of the world stopped too. But the initial aftershock of his death had subsided. The dust had settled, and I longed to feel a sense of normality again. I walked the same walk around the park that we had navigated countless mornings together – down the hill and along the pathway through the trees towards the flower gardens, right and through the play area and past the ponds. I sat by the window of our favourite coffee shop on Stroud Green Road, watching the world go by. I started teaching yoga classes again for the first time since the previous summer. I spoke to my grief coach Marie once a week, I caught up with my friends. And while I was grateful to be able to spend time with them after all those months apart, their company didn't make up for his absence. I craved a kind of intimacy I hadn't experienced for almost a year. It had been seven lonely months since his death, eleven since I'd felt somebody's touch. I wanted to be reminded of what it had felt like to be desired.

In recent weeks, I'd thought about sex often. I'd played out all of the possible scenarios in my head, imagining myself crying halfway through it, forgetting *how* to even do it, or fleeing at the first sight of genitals that weren't Ben's. Guilt tugged at my conscience. How was I supposed to get over him, to just 'move on' to someone else? To do so felt like the worst kind of betrayal. He was my soulmate. I'd said yes when he got down on one knee. I'd hoped that we'd be lucky enough to be granted another fifty years together, and I knew it still wouldn't have felt like long enough. Even if I did find a willing candidate, it was highly unlikely we'd actually get to that part anyway. I was sure they'd get the ick and run for the hills the moment they caught wind of my situation. On paper, I was a spectacularly hot mess. I had a lorry-load of baggage, and not just your usual, run-of-the-mill 'my ex-boyfriend messed me up a bit' kind – I'm talking the 'dead fiancé' kind, someone I just so happened to be completely, utterly, still in love with. He took up every last inch of my heart that there was nothing left to even give. I'd just have to resign myself to an annexe at the bottom of Chloe's garden instead. But was that really it for me? I often wondered. Was my love life really over at thirty?

The doorbell rang, jolting me back to my senses. Chloe was coming over for lunch. Since moving back into the flat, we'd been taking it in turns to visit each other once a week. I ran downstairs to find her standing on the doorstep holding two chai lattes and a brown paper bag in one hand, a small human in the other. 'I bring gifts!' she beamed, pushing strands of hair from her face.

I hugged her tightly and peered inside the bag: *pastel de natas*, still warm. This girl knew the way to my heart. I took my godson Rex from her and grabbed the other end of his pram, burying my head in his baby smell as we climbed the stairs. Chloe's other child, my goddaughter Coralie, was with her partner Mark – Chloe's lucky snog number three. I set myself up on the sofa, Rex bouncing up and down on my knees, while she grabbed a couple of plates from the kitchen.

'I get it, Lotts,' she said, as she sat down on the beanbag opposite me. I'd offloaded the maelstrom of the morning's thoughts onto her the moment she stepped inside the front door. 'I know it's the ultimate head-fuck for you – to not want someone else because all you want is him, but then the idea of being alone is too impossible, so you're obviously thinking about it. God, it's so hard.'

I nodded and took a swig of my chai.

'I think I know what the Ben we know and love would have told you though. He would have told you how deserving you are of love, and he would have given you his blessing to find it again. In fact, I'm sure he would've done that – because that's just the kind of guy he was. He was selfless and wanted the best for everyone, especially you.'

Soon the British government announced travel corridors between certain countries, permitting travel so long as passengers could present a negative PCR test to the airline they were flying with, before leaving and before returning to their home countries.

'Where do you fancy going?' I texted Robyn after the announcement was made on the news one evening. Just before the pandemic, she had moved back home with Harry from Australia. She had a week off at the end of May, in-between finishing her job and starting a new role elsewhere. I scrolled through the list of easyJet destinations on my phone, my thumbs hovering over the capital city of Portugal. 'What about Lisbon?' I suggested. The country had signalled the green light for Brits to visit.

'Yes!' she replied. 'It would be great to get some sun. Let's have a look at flights and get something booked asap.'

On a miserable Wednesday morning a couple of weeks later, we boarded a flight at Stansted airport, north of London, bound for Lisbon. We'd planned to spend the first couple of days in Comporta, a sleepy *freguesia* flanked by carpets of yellow wildflowers, verdant rice paddies and brilliant blue sea an hour south of Lisbon, before driving north again for a weekend in the city. Robyn would fly back to London to start her new job, and I'd stay on for a few days by myself before flying to Ibiza. The urge to visit the island again, to reclaim another piece of myself, had been growing louder lately, and I'd asked Marie in one of our sessions what she thought I should do.

'If it feels exciting for you to contemplate going, contemplate it for a while. Really feel into what it would be like to go. Visualise yourself there. Try to see how it would feel. Here is a kind of litmus test I used a lot early on. Andreas had seven months between his diagnosis and death. I often asked myself: if I knew that I only had seven months left in this world, would I do "the thing" – the trip, the music festival and so on? I really believe in living with complexity after loss. You may decide to go, and feel both excited about it and guilty. I think the key is trusting in your ability to navigate the feelings.' She was right. I could trust myself to navigate whatever the trip would throw at me.

Robyn and I picked up our hire car from the airport and headed south across the bridge over the River Tagus.

'I think I want to have some fun on this trip.' I turned to Robyn in the driver's seat, her chestnut hair whipping in the wind. 'And by fun, I mean I want to meet someone.'

'Oh yeah?' she replied, her eyebrows raised.

'Yeah. Why not?'

I was ready. Widow's fire, it turns out, was a real thing. I had wants that needed tending to, corners of my body that needed to come alive again. It would be strange to kiss someone else's lips, to feel skin against mine that wasn't his – that much was certain. But there was never going to be an ideal time to test the waters, I reasoned. Whether it was months or years down the line, dating after his death was always going to be complicated.

The willing candidate was a sexy Frenchman from Paris called Laurent. We locked eyes on the dance floor of a bar in Bairro Alto, a bustling neighbourhood in Lisbon's city centre. We spent the evening orbiting each other, exchanging flirty glances and conversation. When the lights came on and the music stopped, I gave him my number, and he came over the evening after Robyn left. To my pleasant surprise, I didn't cry. I hadn't forgotten how to do it, and I didn't run away at the first sight of his penis. After a long, drawn-out winter of solitude, to feel the embrace of a tall, dark and handsome stranger was more than welcome. I was desired, after all – Laurent had made that abundantly clear. He said goodbye the morning after and disappeared out the door. *He could have stayed for a coffee*, I thought to myself as I slipped out of bed and into the kitchen to investigate the contents of the fridge. It would have been nice to have had a slightly less abrupt *fin* to our rendezvous – but the night had served the purpose it had intended to serve. We had given each other exactly what the other had needed, and it didn't have to be anything more than that.

The fridge was empty, except for a carton of milk, a handful of salad and half a loaf of stale bread. I showered, threw on a black dress and a pair of sandals and headed outside in search of a cafe for breakfast. As I made my way through the cobbled streets, past the patchwork of ceramic tiles adorning the store fronts and leathery old men chugging on cigars, the corners of my mouth stretched towards my ears. For the first time since Ben died, I felt alive again. So completely, utterly and exquisitely alive, it was as if all my senses had been turned on again one by one. I was holding myself differently, I noticed – chin and chest up, my gaze fixed on the horizon instead of the ground. I was even walking differently, a new lease of life in every step, like I'd finally shaken myself free of the chains that had weighed me down for all those months.

I could live here, I thought to myself as I wandered through the square in Principe Real, a neighbourhood at the top of one of the many hills that overlooked the city. The purple jacaranda trees, the crumbling buildings painted lemon yellow and blushing pink. The outdoor kiosk selling coffee, the farmers' market with fresh Roma tomatoes in crimson red. And the sun-drenched lovers snogging on the grass – a sight that, only a few months ago, would have probably made me want to throw up. *Good for them,* I thought, smiling. Everything felt different here. Lighter, freer, happier. *Better.* And *I* felt lighter, freer, happier, better. The city was undeniably beautiful but, more than that, it was a blank canvas on which I could paint an entirely new life.

It's funny – despite being born in London, it had never really felt like home to me. I'd never felt like I truly belonged. Ben needed to be in London for work, but teaching yoga? I could've done that anywhere, and, honestly, I might have upped sticks a long time ago if I hadn't fallen in love with him. I loved my friends, the nightlife and architecture. The food, the shopping. But all the chaos, the stress? The endless grey skies and rush hour on the Central line? I hated it. All of it. To me, the city was only tolerable if I could occasionally get away. I'd return from a break renewed, only to feel totally fucked again soon after – and so the cycle continued.

I'd tried to live out the same routine in the same place with the same familiar faces, only now, the biggest piece of the puzzle was missing. Every Tube stop, every street corner reminded me of him. Perhaps a part of me had hoped to find him there, to feel closer to him somehow, but instead it only amplified the sound of his absence. I was searching for something that could never be found. There was no escaping my grief, I was aware of that. It would follow me everywhere I went. But I needed to escape the trauma, the memories. I needed to get the hell out of there. What was the worst that could happen, I reasoned, when I'd already lost so much?

◆ ◆ ◆

The next morning, I pulled on a pair of shorts and a t-shirt and headed downstairs, turning left outside the front door and walking as far as my feet would carry me. I wandered through the streets of Baixa-Chiado, past the commercial square by the river and up the hill towards Graça, one of Lisbon's oldest suburbs.

It was a little rustic, a little rundown in parts, but it oozed so much charm that I couldn't help but fall in love with it. Faded pastel facades sprayed with graffiti leaned against each other, jostling for space. Laundry fluttered in the breeze, hanging from the balconies above. I walked past the National Pantheon, a beautiful former seventeenth-century church, and up towards a flea market where rows of bric-a-brac and vintage clothes lay strewn across the concrete. Tables and chairs spilled out of tiny taverns nearby. My stomach growled, and all of a sudden, I was ravenous. I sat down at a tavern on the corner of the park above the market and ordered *bacalhau à brás*, which, according to my floppy-haired and charming waiter, was a traditional dish made from shreds of salted cod, onions and thinly chopped fried potatoes, thrown together with scrambled eggs. I pulled my phone out of my bag and perused a dating app to entertain myself while I waited for my lunch to arrive. I flicked through a sea of profiles, pressing the heart icon on a couple I liked the look of, when a match appeared. His name was Manu, he was twenty-eight years old and a photographer, with big, brown, doe eyes and skin the colour of cappuccino.

We got chatting, and he asked if I wanted to meet him for a drink. It wasn't exactly my usual protocol, sleeping with a guy and then meeting up with another one twenty-four hours later. But what was my motto for the year? Fuck it. What did I stand to lose? Besides, I didn't know anyone in the city. If nothing else, I'd appreciate the company.

'Yeah, sure. Let's do it.'

We planned to meet at the end of my road later that evening, pick up a bottle of wine and go for a walk along the river. After scraping the last few spoonfuls of *bacalhau* from my plate and paying the bill, I ambled back to my flat in Bairro Alto and climbed into bed for a siesta. A few hours later, I pulled on my clothes and put on some make-up, and headed out to meet him. As soon as I got to the front door, my phone pinged.

'I have some bad news,' Manu wrote. 'I'm outside, but one of my friends who I went surfing with yesterday just called me. He has Covid. What should we do? I totally understand if you don't feel comfortable meeting anymore.'

'Hmm. Well, since you're already here, let's just meet and chat at a distance? We can decide what to do from there.'

'Okay, good idea.'

I walked outside to find him leaning against a motorbike on the corner of the road, dressed all in black.

'Hey,' he said coyly as I walked over to him.

'Hello. How are you doing? It's nice to meet you!'

'You too,' he smiled.

We walked along one of the side roads towards a stairwell facing the river.

'You sit over there, and I'll sit here,' I laughed.

We sat down on opposite ends of the stairwell and chatted. He told me he was born and raised in Lisbon. He'd studied multimedia arts at the local university and had worked as a photographer since graduating back in 2014. He was a black belt in jiu jitsu and loved to surf. The conversation flowed effortlessly between us. It struck me how easy he was to talk to, how quickly I felt comfortable around him. He asked me lots of questions and, unlike Laurent, he seemed genuinely interested to know what the answers were.

'So why are you thinking of moving here?'

I hesitated for a moment. I wondered whether or not I ought to tell him the truth. What would he think? Would he run a mile like I'd predicted? Ben's death was so recent, my grief so present still. I couldn't just pretend like none of it had happened.

'Well, I need a fresh start. I was in a relationship for six years – we were engaged, actually. But he died seven months ago. He had stage-four cancer.'

'Oh,' he said, his eyebrows lifting. I could sense he was surprised. *Shit.* I mean, who *wouldn't* be? It's not exactly your standard situation for a thirty-year-old. I searched his face for smears of ick, expecting him to make up an excuse and leave. 'I'm so sorry you went through that,' he offered. 'Wow. That must've been really hard.' To my surprise, he was sweet about it. He asked all the right questions, said all the right things.

For four and a half hours, we sat on the concrete steps talking. There was no bottle of wine, no river, no background music or chatter that might have eased any awkward silences between us. We didn't need any of it because there weren't any. It was just us and a couple of stray cats sniffing around the bins nearby, and it was perfect.

'I wish I could give you a hug or something,' he said as we stood up to leave.

'Me too. I'd have liked that.'

'Let's hang out before you go, if you like?' he said, as we headed back down the road towards my flat. 'I'd really like to see you again.'

I waved him goodbye as he disappeared up the road on his motorbike. I couldn't wipe the smile off my face as I climbed the stairs to the flat. It was the first date in seven years with someone other than Ben, and it wasn't so scary after all.

The following day, we met up again, this time at the park Tapada das Necessidades, west of the city centre. I bought us a *pastel de nata* each from the cafe by the park entrance, and we sat a few metres apart from each other under the jacaranda trees, talking. We wandered south towards the river and along the waterfront, talking some more, occasionally stopping at outdoor kiosks for more snacks.

'I'll be your tour guide when you move here,' he grinned. 'And I'll teach you Portuguese in exchange for English lessons.'

He wanted to take me to Sintra for the day, he said. I'd read about the town online before I arrived. It was nestled high in the hills half an hour north-west. Home to elaborate, colourful palaces and castles, it looked like something out of a fairy tale written by the Grimm brothers. He wanted to teach me how to surf too. I was scared of waves, I told him. The ocean was relatively uncharted territory for most of us Brits. Growing up, I'd only spent a handful of days by the ocean in Cyprus every summer on my family holiday. He laughed, his doe eyes crinkling in the corners. It was a deal. I felt a familiar rush of dopamine that I hadn't felt in a while.

How cute, I thought, as I studied the edge of his heart-shaped mouth. We were already making plans together. But also, *How right.* This couldn't just be a forty-eight-hour thing, no way. All I'd hoped for was for a gorgeous man to entertain me in this gorgeous city for an evening at the very most. But this? I wasn't expecting *this.* He captured my attention. He *was* gorgeous – and he was also smart and funny and, from what I could tell, kind. By the time we parted ways, it was almost midnight. We'd spent eleven and a half hours wandering through the city in our own little world, talking incessantly. We'd talked about our childhoods, our families, our jobs. Our relationships, politics, our goals. I could have continued talking to him for hours and hours – days, in fact – and still leave feeling like I'd barely scratched the surface of him. I wanted to scratch some more. To get right up against it, underneath it even.

The next morning, I flew to Ibiza via Madrid. As the wheels of the plane went down and the ground grew closer, my eyes brimmed with tears. But they weren't sad tears, they were happy ones. Pure and unadulterated, *overjoyed* ones. They poured down my cheeks, like the uncorking of a delicious wine. Here I was, feeling all of the big, difficult feelings like Marie had predicted, doing it anyway. Another plaster ripped off. *If not with him, then for him*, I thought.

Driving to my villa in Portinatx, a former fishing village north of the island, I passed the towns we had driven through together the previous summer, each of them unearthing painful memories that I'd buried somewhere in the deepest caverns of my being. 'But remember the good times,' I reminded myself – the times that came before all the cancer and horror and death. Those were real too; the candlelit dinners surrounded by pink bougainvillea, the moped rides through the countryside, the hikes to secret coves along the coast. One too many tequila shots, dancing under the stars stretched across an obsidian canvas, salty kisses in the sea.

Before, they'd been too agonising to look at. I couldn't for the life of me make sense of the fact that I'd never get to share any of those moments with him again. Quite simply, it *didn't* make any sense – at all. But as I followed the roads that bisected the fields of wildflowers and lush pine forests inland, I couldn't help but smile. It took me by surprise when I glanced in the rear-view mirror and noticed it spread across my face. It hurt to remember, yes. Of course it did. But it felt good too. All of a sudden, I was seized by an over-whelming feeling of gratitude. Perhaps this is just what living with grief would look like: existing in a landscape irrevocably shaped by loss, where every high was tinged with sadness, and every memory imbued with a profound sense of appreciation that the experience had even happened in the first place. What a strange dichotomy of agony and rapture it was. I didn't want those precious memories to remain buried anymore. I wanted to dig them up and lay them flat, pore over them for hours on end. I wanted to remember what it had felt like to be happy, to love and be loved by him. I turned the volume up on the stereo and wound the windows down. A slow, hypnotic beat began blaring from the speakers. *Dum de de dum de de dum dum dum.* This is what it had felt like before. I hung my arm out of the window and let the wind carry it. I breathed in, the invigorating smell of salt and pine filling my nostrils. I pulled into the driveway and bounced over the stones towards the villa when my phone pinged. It was a message from Manu.

'Fancy a phone call?'

I grinned and pressed 'Dial'.

Over the next ten days, I tended to myself with love and care. I took myself on solo dates and ate at our favourite restaurants. I spent time by the ocean, the wordless embrace of the water a healing tonic. And of course – there was Manu. Gorgeous, doe-eyed Manu. He was a welcome distraction from my grief, that much was certain. But he was more than that, I could feel it in my bones. Something kept pulling me towards him. I needed to talk to him, to get to know him more.

19

I returned to London in late June, and the next few weeks passed in a heady whirlwind of fuck it. My best friend Gee managed to coax me back onto the dance floor again one night, inviting me to watch Groove Armada play at Alexandra Palace on a whim just up the road from mine. Over the years, the two of us had spent many mornings step-ball-changing in front of the mirror at dance classes, and countless hours in nightclubs listening to our favourite DJs, so she knew just how scary a prospect it was for me. She held my hand as we made our way through the crowd towards the stage. She reminded me that I could do hard things, that this was a way to honour Ben.

'I've got you babe,' she said, pulling me close, her hazel eyes glinting as the strobe lights passed overhead. 'You're not alone.'

Together with Chloe and Victoria, we indulged in late nights and partying. I was having fun. Things were on the up, I tried to convince myself – but another blow was waiting to kick the air out of my lungs and bring me to my knees again.

I suspected my siblings and I had all been thinking the same thing, it was just that none of us had wanted to actually say the words out loud. The prospect of more illness and grief so soon after losing Ben was unfathomable. 'Surely not,' I'd reasoned, trying to placate my growing unease. Surely we'd had enough bad things happen to be granted a pass – at least for the foreseeable future. But life doesn't really work like that, does it?

In recent months, I'd noticed that my dad's ability to communicate had deteriorated. He'd leave me long, rambling voice notes about nothing in particular, stumbling over his words and losing his train of thought mid-sentence. The pain in his throat that he'd had for the past year had become worse, and he couldn't swallow solid food properly anymore.

'I've got . . . Alzheimer's,' he'd stuttered on the other end of the phone one afternoon in mid-July. 'And oesophageal . . . cancer to boot. What a – what a stroke of luck!' Both diseases were already late stage, he explained, meaning there was very little that could be done to help him. The most we could hope for was that the doctors would be able to extend his life for a bit longer – but how much longer exactly, no one knew.

'Oh, Dad,' I uttered, slack-jawed in disbelief. I was wracked with guilt. It all made sense to me now. I felt we had been growing apart for some time, and I'd avoided his calls in the immediate aftermath of Ben's death, because he hadn't felt like a safe person I could express my grief around and feel comforted by in return. I'd chastised him in secret for not being the dad I'd needed him to be. But of *course* he couldn't be. He was dying, and he needed me. There was no way I could jump ship and leave him like this. Not now. I could go later – Dad on the other hand, wouldn't get a 'later'. And besides, I didn't *want* to leave him. I wouldn't get to undo the things I did, or do the things I didn't do, once he was gone.

Throughout August, Georgia, Oliver and I took it in turns to visit him at his house in Tunbridge Wells every few days. With every visit, he became noticeably more weak. Unable to pass any solid food through his oesophagus, he relied on four high-calorie, fruit-flavoured drinks a day to satiate him. It was a desperately sad sight, but as ever, he took it all in his stride. When I was a baby, he'd undergone intensive chemo and radiotherapy for non-Hodgkin lymphoma. Years later when I was twenty-four, Mum had rushed him to hospital with chest pain. He'd had several heart attacks, and had to have open-heart quadruple bypass surgery to restore four blocked arteries around his heart. Two huge scars ran from his throat to the bottom of his sternum, and from his inner thigh all the way down to his ankle. I never heard him complain.

'What meal are you most looking forward to having again, Dad?' I asked him as I perched on the edge of his chair in his living room, stroking the back of his head. He was due to have a stent fitted in his oesophagus in a couple of weeks' time at the local hospital, that would enable him to eat solid food again.

'Mmm,' he mumbled. 'Well, I'd really like . . . I want to eat some fish and chips again. By the seaside, actually.'

'I love fish and chips,' I answered. I reached over to the box of tissues on the coffee table and pulled one out to wipe the spittle from his chin. 'Why don't we go to Hastings once you've recovered, make a thing of it?'

'Sounds like a plan,' he grinned.

Only things didn't go to plan, and he didn't get to have his fish and chips by the seaside. I'd hoped we might have a few more months of him at the very least, but a week or so after the stent procedure at the start of September, he was admitted to the local hospice for end-of-life care.

One Sunday afternoon a few days after his admission, I sat beside his bed in his room. I held a sponge dripping with melted raspberry ice cream to his lips, brushing the wisps of hair from his forehead with my other hand.

'Mmm,' he murmured, his mouth pulling upwards in a half smile. He let out a hint of a word, unintelligible. He couldn't say more than one at a time by now, and even then it was a challenge.

It must be such an arduous task, dying, I thought to myself. People always said it was the most natural thing in the world, and while that might be true, that didn't mean it was easy.

It certainly seemed that way to me at least. He looked ready, but he was at the mercy of his body. It would take as long as it took for it to shut down. I put the sponge and bowl on the table next to his bed and rested my head on his shoulder. I placed my hand on his chest, his heart beating under his breastbone, laboured and loud. I watched as he lifted his hand to meet mine, moving in slow motion, as if a part of him had already crossed over the threshold towards the Other Side. The energy felt tender between us – as if all that had been left unsaid over the years was reconciled in a single gesture.

'I love you, Daddy,' I told him, my tears soaking his hospital gown.

He grunted. His way of saying it back.

As I lay there with him, my thoughts wandered. I pictured him chasing me, Oliver and Georgia through a maze on the Isle of Wight when I was ten. I thought of all the times he'd pored over the wine and cheese aisles in the *supermarchés* in the Loire Valley on our summer holidays. Even though I was well below the legal drinking age, I could tell it was vitally important not to mess up the pairings of Pinot Noir and Gruyère. I thought of Friday curry nights. His impressive vinyl collection. Him at the front of every Sunday morning yoga class sat on top of ten foam blocks, his knees around his ears. His 3 a.m. alarm on weekends – me on all fours screaming 'DAD!' through the letterbox because I'd forgotten my keys again.

In those quiet moments before death took him, I finally understood something that had escaped me when I was younger. He was my dad, yes – but more than that, he was just another human being, perfectly imperfect, with hopes and dreams and flaws and insecurities like the rest of us. He had done his best, and he had loved me in the way he knew how to. His imminent death, it seemed, was stripping me of my ego, the distortions of 'he said', 'she said', of the importance of being right.

After some time, my brother Oliver came into the room. He kissed me on the forehead and hugged me.

'Go on, girl,' he said, nodding towards the door. 'Make yourself a cup of tea or something and go and get some fresh air. Yeah?'

I nodded and headed out the door and down the corridor towards the communal kitchen. When it came to places to die in, I imagined this was one of the more pleasant ones. Canvas prints of flowers hung from the walls. Fake plants lined the shelves next to reed diffusers that masked the smell of antiseptic. I walked through the conservatory and out into the walled garden, where several of the patients' rooms were obscured behind rows of shrub roses in different shades of apricot and peach. I followed the path to a wooden bench in the far corner and sat down. The garden, I noticed, hummed with life. Two greenfinches were perched on the branch of a nearby birch tree. A cluster of bees were collecting pollen. This was just the way of things: life and death coexisting.

After a while, I walked back inside and settled into the sofa in the corner of Dad's room, watching as Oliver chatted to him, occasionally running a flannel over his skin to keep him cool. The late afternoon sun poured through the shutters, casting his frail body in golden light. A tear ran down my face.

'I'm not going anywhere if you want to go home, sis,' Oliver said, his voice soothing. 'I'll be by his side, don't worry.'

We stood up and hugged again. I told Dad I loved him one last time and left. He died six days after losing consciousness, on 13th September.

◆ ◆ ◆

The medium, Rebecca, had told me that I'd meet Ben's soul brother far sooner than I'd expected to. She'd said that I'd recognise him. It was late September, and I'd come to suspect that Manu was the soul brother in question. Since leaving Lisbon in June, we'd spoken almost every day on the phone. Sometimes our calls lasted hours, and even then, they never felt like long enough. The conversation between us was so vast and effortless, it seemed almost inexhaustible. When the time came to hang up each call, I was always left wanting more.

'Maybe I should ask Ben for a sign,' I said to myself one morning as I scrolled through Dad's funeral checklist with a cup of tea in hand. I'd made a habit of speaking to Ben in my head or out loud in recent months. He had always given me valuable guidance, and why should it stop now? I needed it from him more than ever now he wasn't here.

My friend Georgie always asked her late partner Lachie to send her owls. In the book *Signs: The Secret Language of the Universe* by Laura Lynne Jackson, I'd read that the more specific we were when asking a loved one for a sign, the less likely we were to question it. Unlike something generic like a feather or a rainbow, owls were specific enough for Georgie not to question the sign whenever one appeared – and they *always* did, in the most random situations and places. Lach was still around her, loving and supporting her beyond this realm.

'Okay, then,' I muttered under my breath as I wandered past the pond in Finsbury Park, kicking up the leaves into a brilliant array of orange, yellow and red. 'Benny, if Manu is the soul brother, I'm going to need you to send me a sign. Please send me an owl.' I could count on one hand the number of times I'd ever seen an owl in real life. Most of them were nocturnal. What were the chances of coming across one in the middle of London?

The following day, I set off early to catch the train to Chloe's in Carshalton, south London. It was my turn to visit her. I pushed through the front door an hour or so later to find her standing in the kitchen with Coralie and Rex hanging off her legs. I put the kettle on and sifted through the cupboards for snacks as she attended to the babes, when up popped a message from Manu on my phone. He was on holiday with his friend Afonso in Vila Nova de Cacela, in the south-west corner of Portugal.

'Hey,' he wrote. 'I've been thinking about you all morning.'

I smiled and leaned against the kitchen counter.

'Hello, you. Me too. What have you been up to?'

'Well, apart from thinking about you, just relaxing. We're about to head out for lunch now. And get this – we saw an owl at the beach this morning. I've never seen one in real life before. I'll send you a picture of it – so random.'

'What the *fuck*?' I mouthed as I poured hot water into two ceramic cups. I put the kettle down and read the message again. I read it a few more times, just to make sure I wasn't imagining things. *We saw an owl at the beach.*

I got the milk out of the fridge and clicked on the photo he sent me, when a shiver shot through my spine. Staring directly into the camera in front of a beach patrol car on the sand, was a big brown owl with round orange eyes. The patrol team, Manu told me, had swum out with a surfboard to rescue it. It couldn't take flight, and was being dragged further out to sea.

I stirred in the milk and stared at the picture, astounded.

'What is it?' Chloe asked.

Rex waddled over to me and tugged at the hem of my jeans, burbling something indiscernible.

'Take a look at this.' Passing her my phone, I scooped Rex up and told her about the sign I'd asked for the day before.

'Sorry, what?' She looked at me and then looked at the phone again, her jaw almost on the floor. 'Oh my God . . .' Her voice trailed off.

'I know,' I breathed. She knew exactly what it meant. My heart welled. Ben had heard me loud and clear. He had sent the sign I had asked for, delivered to me first-hand by the subject of my question. Manu was indeed the soul connection, and Ben had given me his blessing to love again.

20

In the days leading up to Dad's funeral on 8th October, a kind of numbness took up residence inside my body. I was catapulted yet again into the throes of joint executor duties. I had another funeral to arrange, another life to shut down, another estate to sort with Oliver and Georgia. I barely cried. To be honest, I barely felt anything at all. My grief for Ben eclipsed everything.

At first, I wondered if there was something wrong with me. I wondered if my inability to express any emotion over Dad's death was a reflection of how challenging our relationship had been at times. But it wasn't that. I came across a phrase for it online one day: cumulative grief. It happens when you don't have time to process one loss – whether it be the loss of a loved one, your business, your home or something else – before you incur another. Scientists, I'd read, were beginning to recognise the experience of loss as a specific type of trauma. It reorganises the way the mind and brain manage perceptions. It changes not only how we think and what we think about, but also our very capacity to think. It impairs our ability to function properly, making the most basic survival and defence mechanisms a priority above anything else.

It made sense, then, that if I was to continue functioning with any semblance of normality, I couldn't possibly process both losses at once. My mind, brain and body were only capable of carrying so much. Besides, I didn't actually have any time to grieve – I had a move abroad to organise. Dad's death had turned the 'fuck it' motto I'd adopted earlier in the year up a notch. I'd told myself that I couldn't possibly move abroad while he was terminally ill, that I would only do it after he'd died. So why kick the can down the road and delay it any longer? 'It's either now or never,' I told myself the morning after his funeral.

I sat down at my dining table after breakfast and booked a one-way flight to Lisbon, leaving on 27th October. Which, I suddenly realised, left me with just under three weeks to sort through the entirety of Ben's belongings and clear out the flat. Exactly eighteen days to pack up all thirty-six years of his life, and the last seven years of mine. I looked around the living room. What was I supposed to do with it? Should I hold on to all of it, some of it, or *none* of it? Where would I even begin? When met with her overwhelm over the years, Jaz's mum Oeda had always responded with the same question. 'How do you eat an elephant?' she'd ask her.

One bite at a time.

I walked over to the bookcase next to the sofa and pulled a few of his books down – *Magicians of the Gods* by Graham Hancock, *The Prophet* by Kahlil Gibran, Aldous Huxley's *Brave New World*. I flicked through their worn pages. He'd loved reading as much as I had. He'd had an insatiable hunger to discover more about the world, to experience life through the lens of somebody else who could teach him something new. A friend had sent him *The Prophet* in the post after learning about his terminal diagnosis. I could pay it forward. I could give his belongings a second life. And anyway, Ben was not his clothes or his books. I didn't need to hold on to them to validate our love or my grief. I pulled the rest of the books down from the shelf and put them into two boxes – ones to keep for myself, and ones to give away. I poured the contents of our wardrobe and chests of drawers onto the bedroom floor, separating out two piles of clothes to give to charity, and clothes to keep. Over the next fortnight, with the help of Oliver, Jen, and my mum and Dougal, I filled fourteen bags of rubbish to take to the dump, and half a dozen suitcases to take to Lisbon. The rest, I scattered across every charity shop within a mile.

◆　◆　◆

On the morning of my flight, I wandered through an empty flat, thinking of all the life that had been lived inside its walls. The side-splitting laughter, the ecstasy of making love. All of the merciless terror and pain and grief. I thought of all the life that *ought* to have been lived – our marriage, our firstborn. I knew I couldn't continue to stand still, longing for things that existed only in my imagination. To do so would be to torment myself needlessly. Time kept passing, the world kept spinning and people kept moving forwards. What else could be done, but to keep moving too?

My friend Victoria came over to give me a hug goodbye and wave me off. I took some deep breaths, walked out of the front door, and locked it behind me.

'Fuck me, these suitcases are heavy,' she chortled as we lugged them down the stairs. 'What on earth have you got in them?' I laughed. 'In all seriousness though, Lottster, I'm so proud of how far you've come. You're doing a brave and amazing thing, moving abroad. And I can't wait to visit you.' She was a sensitive soul, Vic, like me. She had a knack for reading non-verbal cues and knowing when a difficult moment called for humour. I gave her a hug and we stood on the kerb together, chatting while we waited for my taxi to arrive. I did feel brave. And I felt empowered – more empowered than I'd ever felt in my life. I was walking away from all that felt familiar and safe, towards the unknown – heart open, head first.

When I landed at Lisbon airport six hours later, Manu was waiting for me at Arrivals. I walked down the ramp towards him, all six suitcases balancing precariously on a trolley. My heart pounded inside my chest as his eyes met mine and we waved at each other from across the hall. Would it be as good as I'd imagined it to be between us? I asked myself. Or had I made him out to be something he wasn't? Was it all just wishful thinking, an attempt to run away from my pain?

We hugged and there I was, in his arms at last. I drank in the smell of his cologne, a burst of citrusy notes with a woody, patchouli undertone.

'I'm so happy you're finally here,' he grinned shyly.

'Me too.'

We loaded my suitcases into the boot of his car, and drove half an hour across town to São Bento, a quiet neighbourhood ten minutes down the hill from the square in Principe Real. The room I'd rented for the first few months was on the fifth floor of an old building covered in cobalt blue tiles. We carried my suitcases up the steep, rickety staircase and dumped them inside the doorway to the flat. My bedroom on the left was pokey and unclean, with just a single clothes rail and a mattress on the floor.

Uh-oh, I thought as I glanced around the room. *Have I made a big mistake?*

'You can totally make this work,' Manu assured me.

I thought I'd done well to conceal the disappointment on my face.

'Don't worry – it's not for long.'

He was right. *Be rational, Lotte.* I couldn't get cold feet already. I'd barely stepped off the bloody plane. This was merely a stopgap, an in-between place until I found my new home. It would have to do for now.

I unpacked a few suitcases and freshened up while Manu ran a few errands. A couple of hours later, once the sun had disappeared behind the terracotta rooftops, he picked me up on his motorbike and drove me to a restaurant for some dinner. It was a no-frills sort of joint, with paper tablecloths, harsh lighting and waiters who didn't care to hide the fact that they'd have rather spent their evenings somewhere else. I watched as Manu made an incision at the tail end of our roasted sea bass, before running the flat edge of his knife along the spine. I studied him as he pulled tiny bones from the flesh, made note of all the ways he wasn't Ben.

But he's not Ben, I tried to reason with myself – he was different, and being different wasn't necessarily a bad thing.

After dinner, we paid the bill and went for a drive through the city, up and down the hills, round the winding, cobbled lanes past the pastel-coloured buildings. And there it was again, I noticed. The dichotomy of agony and rapture. I ought to have been overjoyed, and I was – I was back in this gorgeous city, pressed up against this gorgeous man. But I was sad too, for all that I had left behind to get here. I felt myself pushing and pulling in opposite directions, walking the threshold again between two worlds: the land of the living and the land of the dead.

We parked his bike outside the entrance to my building some time later and headed upstairs. His doe eyes unstitched me in the doorway to my bedroom, and I melted into his arms and into bed like butter. I could feel his touch beginning to reassemble the broken parts of me that I'd salvaged amidst the rubble. What would Ben make of all this, of me falling for somebody else? I was confused. Wasn't this technically cheating? I tried to silence the voice that kept telling me that Ben was standing over my bed, watching us. Perhaps it was better to quit while I was ahead, to cut myself off and buffer the pain that would follow if – or rather when – it ended. How could I possibly love somebody again, knowing all that there was to lose? But I was already in too deep, I realised. I had feelings for him – big ones.

A few weeks later marked the first anniversary of Ben's death: 14th November 2021. I'd been holding out for it, as though it would feel like reaching some sort of finish line, by which point I could declare myself done grieving. For the past year, I'd counted, almost obsessively, how many days, weeks and months it had been since he had died, making a concerted effort to wallow in my anguish every time the date of the fourteenth appeared. I'd attempted to numb the pain by whatever means necessary. I'd done what I thought I'd needed to do to heal, and I'd checked off all the boxes. I'd moved to a new home in a new country. I'd built a grief community online. I was going out and meeting people and making new friends. I had therapy once a week with Marie, and spoke about my feelings openly. I'd even met somebody else. And I'd come to accept Ben's death in that I didn't fight against it anymore. By all accounts, I was 'doing well'. But reaching the year mark didn't make my grief magically disappear. I woke up that morning and I was *still* grieving, because – spoiler alert! – he was still dead.

Clearly then, everything I'd heard about the grieving process – how it followed a linear, upwards trajectory of six stages, from denial, anger, bargaining and depression, to acceptance and, finally, meaning – was bollocks. I'd felt all of those things, my God had I. You're damn right I felt angry about Ben dying. Actually, more than that – I felt furious. Furious at his doctors, furious at anyone who dared to moan about how the pandemic had ruined their summer holiday and wedding plans. Sometimes, I even felt furious at him. *How could he have left me in such a sorry state?* I'd catch myself thinking. I'd bargained with his death a thousand times, tried to negotiate with a higher power to bring him back somehow. I'd thought that maybe if I had done more – sent more emails, done more research, advocated harder – he would still be here. But it certainly wasn't one thing or the other, transitioning between each stage with grace and ease. I could swing from rage, disbelief and overwhelm to a bursting-at-the-seams kind of gratitude on any given day. It was constantly up and down, two step forwards, one back. Grief, as far as I could see, was a messy and unpredictable soup of countless states and emotions that came in varying shapes and sizes.

Of course I wasn't done grieving, I realised, as I wandered through Baixa-Chiado with a friend in search of lunch. And actually, I was okay with that. I didn't want to not feel my grief. It was a reflection of all the love I had to give to him that I no longer could. It showed me that our relationship had meant something, and meant something still. But was I going to continue compounding my pain, the sum of my life a series of moments I simply 'got through' until I died too? I didn't want to live like that, not anymore.

As I watched the sun drop below the horizon from the Miradouro viewpoint in Graça, it dawned on me: no amount of partying and impulsive spending, no amount of community, friends, therapy – or even time – would heal my grief in its entirety. I couldn't run from it, I couldn't get rid of it. I could only grow around it.

21

'You know I love you, right?' said Manu.

We were sitting side by side at my dining table, huddled together against the damp December air. He'd spent the past hour toiling in the kitchen, cooking pan-fried salmon, sweet potato purée and a fig and goat's cheese salad. He'd even decorated the table, complete with candles and a bouquet of flowers in all my favourite colours. I nodded and kissed him. I did know, and I knew I felt the same way about him – but the more time we'd spent together in recent weeks, the more my guilt and confusion spiralled. I knew I was clinging to certain stories – that I was undermining Ben's death and letting him go by being with somebody else. That if I allowed myself to fully give and receive love again, then ours no longer meant as much. I'd made excuses not to attend things he'd invited me to. I'd held him at arm's length, avoided introducing him to my new friends.

'I do,' I replied. 'I just need time. Just give me some more time.'

A few days later on 23rd December, he dropped me off in the Departures car park at Lisbon airport where I'd catch a flight to Cancun on the east coast of Mexico to meet my friend Georgie. We'd decided to boycott the second Christmas without Ben and Lachie together and travel around Mexico for three weeks. I'd thought about what it would feel like to go back to the place he had died, and while it was home to some of the worst conceivable memories, it was also home to some of the best – which was partly why he'd been so enthusiastic about returning for treatment. It would be painful, yes, but over the last thirteen months, I'd learned that avoiding things that were connected to him wouldn't make that pain disappear. I wanted to usher in memories of the good times, climbing Aztec ruins together, dancing through the streets to mariachi musicians and eating tacos. I wanted to rewrite the story and reclaim parts of Mexico for myself.

I landed in the early hours, pulled my suitcase off the carousel in the baggage reclaim area, and climbed into the back of a taxi headed for our hostel in downtown Cancun.

'Lod-ee!' came Georgie's soft, caramel voice from the darkness as I walked up the steps towards the entrance to greet her.

'You're real!' I gasped as we hugged each other. After almost a year of being pen pals, we were finally together. 'I can't believe we're meeting for the first time.'

'I know,' she said, grinning. 'It's like I've known you my whole life!'

I smiled back at her. I felt the same. Nobody knew my pain like Georgie did. She'd pulled me out of some of my darkest moments and vice versa. We'd spent countless hours on the phone, each of us taking it in turns to convince the other one to not give up. After a quick shower and a bite to eat, I flopped into bed next to her and fell asleep.

The following morning, woken up at the crack of dawn by jet lag, we threw on some clothes and took a taxi two hours south to Tulum, a bohemian coastal town surrounded by Mayan ruins, crystal-clear cenotes and dense jungle. We dumped our bags at our hotel and wandered through town towards one of the local gyms to shake off the travel, retracing the same steps that Ben and I had made four years earlier. Just past the gym's reception desk stood a wooden barrel full of water and ice. Georgie and I glanced at each other, both grinning, as if to say, 'Shall we?'

I'd read that the benefits of freezing your tits off were substantiated by scientific evidence. Supposedly, our ability to withstand the stress of the cold could help us to adapt to and manage other, unrelated stressors in a process called cross-adaptation. In other words, it enhanced our resilience, our capacity to withstand and to bounce back from challenging experiences. I'd read about the Dutch athlete Wim Hof, whose first wife Marivelle-Maria had died by suicide in 1995 after jumping off an eight-storey building. Cold water had helped him to heal from his loss. He went on to break numerous Guinness World Records, including the world record for the furthest swim under ice at 57.5 metres in 2000, and the longest full-body immersion in ice at 1 hour, 53 minutes and 2 seconds in 2013. I didn't have any great ambitions to set a world record by any stretch of the imagination, but I was curious to find out whether it could aid my recovery. Until now, so much of my grieving process had been cerebral – a lot of thinking and feeling and talking and writing. But there was only so much those things could do. I needed to get out of my head more and into my body. I needed to dig up the trauma that remained lodged there, shake it out.

We changed into our bikinis and without giving it too much thought, quickly clambered into the barrel. I gasped as soon as my feet hit the water. The pain was searing, like a thousand needles perforating my skin, pulled tight over my muscles like a rubber band. I willed myself to hold on for a minute, aided by long, laboured breaths and a pep talk from Georgie.

'Go on, Lotts,' she cried. 'Just breathe. I believe in you, old girl!'

I observed the thoughts that came and went. *I can't do this! Wait . . . Maybe I can. Only another thirty seconds? Okay, I've got this. Shit! No, I haven't. Twenty left? Okay . . . Maybe I have.*

How many times had I talked myself out of doing something on the basis that it was too hard? It was not that it was too hard, I suddenly realised – it was that I'd told myself I couldn't do it. I'd given up. There were hard things in life. Receiving a terminal diagnosis was one of them. Enduring months of the most aggressive chemotherapy drug on the market, knowing there was a chance it might not work and you'd end up dying anyway was another. *Get a grip, Lotte,* I told myself. Submerging myself in cold water was not hard.

Once the minute was up, the effects were in full swing. We jumped out of the barrel to a group of boisterous Americans in offensively tight budgie-smugglers high-fiving us. I felt exhilarated. Unstoppable. I'd conquered that silly inner voice that had tried to sabotage me, that had told me, 'I can't'. There was really no such thing as 'can't' – only a perceived limitation in my mind.

On Christmas Day, we returned to the gym for a second ice plunge and a workout, before heading to the beach for coconut ceviche, nachos, guacamole and fresh prawns, washed down with a couple of spicy margaritas in Ben and Lachie's honour. It was a far cry from the Christmas before that had gone by barely noticed, indistinguishable from all of the other days that had passed since he died. As we sat in the sand together, watching the sun drop towards the horizon, I turned to her. 'It's funny, you know – even with all of this grief, this might just be one of the best Christmases I've ever had.'

Eager to escape the throngs of party-goers descending upon Tulum, on New Year's Eve we headed further south to Bacalar, a small town near the Belize border. We would welcome in the first morning of 2022 at a beautiful hotel overlooking Bacalar Lagoon. The hotel seemed to emerge from the sand and Yucatan palms as if birthed from nature itself, a seamless mixture of wood, stone, linen and earthy kilim. The lagoon was known by locals, we were told, as *la Laguna de los Siete Colores* – the lagoon of the seven colours. The depth of the water, the sand and limestone, along with myriad minerals and algae, created seven distinct shades of blue and turquoise that changed depending on the time of day. We woke up before dawn on 1st January, and sat on the decking outside. As the sun rose over the silhouette of mangroves in the distance, the water glittered like liquid gold. I sat and watched in silence: the kingfishers and dragonflies skimming across the water's surface. My thoughts, my feelings. The other hotel guests gliding about in quiet reverence for the new year that stretched ahead.

And so came the burning question from somewhere in my mind: who was I, without him? And what would my life look like now?

I knew that connections are what give life meaning. Our loved ones help to lay the foundations our lives are built upon. They help to shape us. What happens, then, when they are taken away? When their absence strips us bare of everything we've ever believed made us who we are? I'd had a fairly good idea of who I was before I met Ben. Well, as good an idea as anyone who'd spent a mere twenty-four years on the planet would have. But the deeper I fell in love, the more I became tangled up in him, the more I lost my sense of self. I'd relied on him to validate my lovability and worth. I had built so much of my identity around our relationship, and his death had blown it to smithereens. Parts of me went with him that I was sure could never be salvaged. *And maybe*, I thought, *it's meant to be that way.* Those parts belonged to a version of me that existed when he was here – *only* because he was here. And that felt kind of beautiful.

In the early days after he died, I'd felt as though I had nothing else to grasp on to besides my grief. I wore it like a badge of honour pinned to my chest. I told anyone and everyone willing to listen, 'I have a fiancé, his name's Ben, he died.' I wanted to brand it across my face, shout from the top of my lungs, 'I'm widowed! I'm griev-ing!' I told myself that so *long* as I was grieving, I was honouring him. That my grief was what kept us connected. But neither of those things were true – or at least, they were only partly true. I could see that now. Honouring him was not limited to sobbing on the bathroom floor, writhing about in anguish. I honoured him by dancing to our favourite music. I honoured him every time I ate a cheese sandwich, a bag of crisps. I honoured him by being kind, by letting my joy spill out of me, unchecked. Our love, my precious memories, and all the ways he continued to change my life, even in death, meant we would never be ripped apart again.

I would always be his partner, and I would always be a grieving person, I realised – that much was certain. But I was so much more than that too. I was a human being, continually learning and evolv-ing, perfectly imperfect and whole and complete, with or *without* him. I'd survived for twenty-four years before we'd met each other, which meant that, perhaps, I could survive again. I was his partner and a grieving person, yes. And I was an introverted extrovert too. I was a nature lover, a lover of non-fiction and documentaries. A logophile and psychonaut. I was highly sensitive, passionate and curious, a glass-half-full sort of person. I felt most alive on a dance floor. I loved dirty jokes and deep conversations. I was kinder and wiser because of him. I knew what it meant to love and be loved. And I would make the most of this life of mine while I still had the chance. What did that look like? I hadn't a clue. But I would savour it, like the sweetness of a ripe mango on my tongue. I would suck the nectar from my fingers, lick the plate clean.

◆ ◆ ◆

A few days later, Georgie and I travelled east to Tepoztlán, a bucolic town in the heart of Mexico nestled between giant copper-coloured mountains. Our days were spent drifting between the restaurant of our hotel, the freshwater pool in the walled garden, and the treatment rooms in the spa. We talked about Ben and Lachie incessantly, shared memories and dreamed up ideas for all the ways we planned to honour them. Fundraisers, charities – books, even. We set goals for the year ahead. We checked out the following Tuesday and hailed a taxi to drive us an hour north to our final stop, Mexico City. As the road signs for the city centre came into view, I wondered whether memories would come flooding back, my grief all fresh and raw again. But they were just memories, I reminded myself. That was then, and this was now. I could feel safe again in the now. We strolled through the Bosque de Chapultepec park and along the tree-lined avenues of Polanco before looping back towards Roma Norte, the same places I'd visited with his ashes in tow thirteen months before. The pain was there, I noticed. But it was different. Before, it had felt razor sharp and all-consuming. Now? It was softer now, like a dull ache.

On a humid Tuesday morning, I hugged Georgie goodbye at the airport and began my journey back to Lisbon via Cancun. Manu offered to pick me up at Arrivals again once I'd landed. As the plane left the ground, I wondered, maybe my capacity to love was boundless. What if this was my chance to experience love again, only with somebody different? To build the life I had dreamed of that had disappeared with Ben?

Human beings are complex creatures, capable of carrying many different things at once. We don't love one best friend any more than our other best friend. A parent doesn't love their second child any less than their first. Wasn't it entirely plausible then, that my heart was big enough to love two people at once?

There was only one way to find out.

Epilogue

A lot has happened since then. The last couple of years have rounded the edges of my pain. These days the darkness seldom flares up, and when it does, it's only fleeting. Don't be mistaken though – I miss Ben a lot. It hurts to think of all the suffering he endured. I grieve for the life that was stolen from him, and every so often I find myself wondering what could have been. Regulating my hypervigilance is a daily practice, and one I've yet to master. I witnessed a rapacious and unforgiving disease devour an otherwise healthy thirty-six-year-old for months on end, only to watch someone else succumb to the same type of disease less than a year later. It takes a lot of work to drown out the voice in my head that tells me that more bad things are going to happen, that another loved one is next. I miss my family and friends in London. My life looks radically different to what it looked like back then, but it's a beautiful one all the same.

I've come to realise that just because life doesn't unfold how we expect it to, it doesn't mean that what comes next is necessarily bad or worse. While good things can fall away, other good things can take up the space that those good things once occupied. And truth be told, there are elements of my life now that are better than my life before. Back then, I was adrift, teaching yoga, a job my heart was never really in, doing things I thought I was supposed to do, for the sake of it. I played small and blended in, afraid of what might happen if I was to allow myself to be fully seen. I never really felt at home in London. I tried to make it work for seven years but, well, I was a square peg in a round hole. Instead, Ben became my home. I relied on him for my sense of footing in the world.

But now? Now I write for a living, and while there are days where words don't come so easily, it enriches my soul in ways very few other things do. My purpose has never felt more clear to me: I am here to write, to create, to help people.

I'm still living in Lisbon. It's been the perfect place for me to heal and rebuild. The summers here seem to last forever. The drop in temperature come wintertime is cushioned by the beautiful colours splashed across every building. The cadence of the city suits me, a sort of relaxed amble where nothing gets done in a rush – not so different to the *mañana mañana* philosophy followed by our Spanish neighbours to the east. Home, I've realised, is no longer limited to one person or to a single set of coordinates on a map. It is found in hugs with loved ones, in my mum's kitchen. It is found beneath the trees in Sintra, along the beaches in Aljezur. It is on dance floors, in my best friends' laughs. And perhaps most importantly, I have found a home within myself. So long as I'm alive, that cannot be taken from me, no matter how violent the storm that threatens to uproot it. I've found healing here. I've made new friends for life. And against all expectations, I've even found love. Oh – and that no-frills joint with paper tablecloths, terrible lighting and equally terrible waiters? It's one of my favourites now.

Speaking of love, I wish I could tell you that Manu and I rode off into the sunset together and lived happily ever after, only it hasn't been quite as simple as that. It's been a long and sometimes painful journey, with lots of bumps and U-turns, even a break-up somewhere in-between. Yet despite all the ways I tried to push him away, he loved me anyway, steady and unfaltering.

I almost didn't include the bits about dating again, you know. I was worried about what others would think – that it was too soon, that I don't love Ben as much as I say I do, or that I must be over my grief. But I've learned that grief doesn't work like that. There is no such thing as moving on, there is only moving forwards. Eventually, I learned to relinquish the guilt and let Manu in. It's not the same, no, but I think that being different is a good thing.

Nobody told me the truth about grief. About the wild, unbridled force of it. About how it alters your DNA, rearranges your insides. Nobody told me about the quiet sorrow that sinks into the substrate of your awareness. They didn't tell me that it forces you to live in a landscape forever marred by the knowing that there will be more loss and heartbreak to come. But what they also didn't tell me was that gratitude could burst forth unexpectedly from the silt like flowers in bloom. That grief could catalyse a sort of ecstatic aliveness, where every day, every moment would be held sacred.

I know I'll see Ben again someday. This is just one chapter of an eternal love story. But until then, I vow to make lemonade from the lemons life has given me, no matter how bittersweet it tastes. For myself? Absolutely. But also for Ben, and for other loved ones I've lost. Because they no longer get to.

ACKNOWLEDGEMENTS

This book owes itself in its entirety to Ben, without whom it wouldn't have existed in the first place. I'm so lucky to have known your love. Thank you for choosing me, for shaping me into the woman I am. I promised you that I would tell our story one day and I hope I have made you proud.

I couldn't have wished for a better agent, the brilliant Megan Staunton at Bergstrom Studio, who slid into my DMs many moons ago asking if I'd ever thought about writing a book. Thank you for believing in me long before I did, and for reading countless iterations of my book proposal with steadfast enthusiasm and patience – many of which were rather shit, let's be honest. You've guided me through this process with compassion and clarity, and it's been a total joy to work with you. And to the equally brilliant Abigail Bergstrom, whose career and work I truly admire. It's the greatest honour to be on a roster alongside so many incredible writers.

Thank you to my fabulous editor Victoria Haslam, for opening the door and giving me this extraordinary, life-changing opportunity. You pulled a different story out of the proposal – the one I wanted to tell the most. And to my editor Sam Boyce, who inspired me to rethink the early drafts of the manuscript – your input and encouragement have been invaluable.

Thank you to my incredible mum Angi, for your relentless love, devotion, generosity and support over the last thirty-three years, and for putting me back together again after losing Ben. A few years ago, you told me that there was a story inside of me, waiting to be written. Thank you for planting the seed and continuing to nurture it. I am who I am because of you and I love you beyond words.

Thank you to my siblings: to my sweet sister Georgia, for your wisdom and unwavering support. You are an angel in human form and I love doing life by your side. And to my darling brother Oliver, for always being in my corner. Where would I be without the two of you? It's impossible to imagine. Thank you to my step-dad Dougal, for your indispensable guidance and outrageous jokes. And to my dear dad Steve, for all the lessons you taught me. Thank you to Manu, for boarding this crazy roller coaster ride and refusing to get off, even when things got hard.

To two-thirds of the sacred triangle, Chloe Mackenzie and Jaz O'Hara. Chlo, thank you for your unconditional love and radical honesty. Jaz, for your devotional, compassionate spirit, and for quite literally carrying me through those early days. Love you both forever.

A special thank you to my beautiful friend and one of the kindest souls I've ever met, Annie Clempner Clarke. Thank you to Gee Coppen, Robyn Eacott, Will Clempner Clarke, Lauren Fraser, and Victoria Williams. Thank you to my amazing Lisbon friends who have held me as I reimagine my life again – especially Richy Elliott, and Geri Kinde and Jenna Scott. You guys put the silver in silver linings! Thank you to my grief coach Marie Goudreau, and to my grief sisters Ellidy Pullin and Georgie Copeland. Thank you to my trusted friend and fellow writer Jess Mills, and to my mentor, ally and friend, Jay Cat James. Your support and solidarity have played a crucial role in my recovery. A heart-felt thank you to Ben's wonderful mum, Jean.

I'm eternally grateful for the ongoing support from the music industry, particularly Ben's colleagues and friends at CAA. A special mention to the great and powerful Jen Hammel and Maria May who inspire me to no end.

Last but not least, to the countless gorgeous strangers who have continued to support me from afar, and to those navigating grief. This book is as much for you as it is for me. Thank you. I hope it helps you in some way.

ABOUT THE AUTHOR

Photo © 2023 Manuel Barbosa

Lotte Bowser was born in London in 1990. After graduating from the University of Nottingham with a 2:1 in French Studies, she worked in TV and music production before pursuing a career as a yoga teacher.

Acting as primary caregiver to her fiancé Ben, and navigating her way through the subsequent grief following his death in 2020, Lotte turned to her social media platform to bring awareness to the taboo subjects of death, loss and grief, building a community of tens of thousands of followers. In 2021 she co-wrote a digital workbook called *Now What? A Guide to Navigating Life After Loss* to support people experiencing bereavement. She has written well-being and lifestyle features for *Women's Health*, ITV's *Woo*, and *Refinery29*, and has featured in *Harper's Bazaar*, the *Express* and the *Mirror*.

Follow the Author on Amazon

If you enjoyed this book, follow Lotte Bowser on Amazon to be notified when the author releases a new book!

To do this, please follow these instructions:

Desktop:

1) Search for the author's name on Amazon or in the Amazon App.

2) Click on the author's name to arrive on their Amazon page.

3) Click the 'Follow' button.

Mobile and Tablet:

1) Search for the author's name on Amazon or in the Amazon App.

2) Click on one of the author's books.

3) Click on the author's name to arrive on their Amazon page.

4) Click the 'Follow' button.

Kindle eReader and Kindle App:

If you enjoyed this book on a Kindle eReader or in the Kindle App, you will find the author 'Follow' button after the last page.